ROLL UP, ROLL UP!

FOR THE MOST SPECTACULAR SHOW ON EARTH!

TOP GEAR

COMING TO A TOWN NEAR YOU THROUGHOUT THE SUMMER OF 1897

FEATURING

Mr Jeremiah Clarkson's Incredible Perambulator

WATCH IN AMAZEMENT AS HE ACHIEVES UN~NATURAL SPEED IN EXCESS OF 12 MILES~PER~HOUR!

THE DIMINUTIVE MR RUDYARD HAMMOND

A MAN SO SMALL HE IS BARELY VISIBLE TO THE NAKED EYE!

THE FACIAL~TOPIARY STYLINGS OF LORD MAY

MARVEL AT THE INCREDIBLE AMOUNT OF TIME HE TAKES TO APPLY HIS MOUSTACHE WAX!

INCLUDING ALL THEIR MOST POPULAR SAYINGS

"HOW MANY VICISSITUDES CAN BE PLACED IN OUR PATH BEFORE EMBARKING UPON THIS ENDEAVOUR?"

"THE OUTCOME OF THIS UNDERTAKING HAS NOT BEEN FELICITOUS!"

"UPON THE RECEIPT OF THAT MOST EXPLOSIVE INFORMATION WE MUST MAKE HASTE!"

TOP GEAR

Ambitious… yet profoundly failing to avail itself of any desirable outcome

WHAT PEOPLE SAID ABOUT THE LAST
BIG BOOK OF TOP GEAR

'I laughed so hard one of my arms literally fell off' – **Jeremy Clarkson**

'*On The Edge: My Story* by Richard Hammond is still available in all good bookshops' – **Richard Hammond**

'I liked the part where it talked about carburettor needle valves' – **James May**

'Then one of my kidneys literally fell off its mountings' – **Jeremy Clarkson**

'The follow up to *On The Edge: My Story*, entitled *As You Do: Adventures with Evel, Oliver and the Vice President of Botswana*, is also out in paperback, priced £7.99' – **Richard Hammond**

'Oh, hello. May here again. Sorry, I thought you said "What did I think of the *Haynes Repair Manual for the Triumph 2000?*"' – **James May**

'And my head exploded. Literally exploded. Literally' – **Jeremy Clarkson**

'You can order both books online, and why not take that chance to also buy *Richard Hammond's Car Science*. It's a great way to teach your kids about the science of cars, and much, much more!' – **Richard Hammond**

'Erm, hello. It's May again. Sorry about this. I should have said that I quite liked *The Big Book of Top Gear*, but not as much as the *Haynes Repair Manual for the Triumph 2000*' – **James May**

WHAT PEOPLE SAID ABOUT
THE *HAYNES REPAIR MANUAL*
FOR THE TRIUMPH 2000

'Hilarious!' – **James May**

Strange taste p62

p20

p14

Strange man

Strange smell

p90

Strange touch

p22

Win!
A luxury trip to
Surrey worth £24!

p113

This Week

FREE NIGEL HAVERS FOR EVERY READER!
SEE NIGEL HAVERS FOR DETAILS

OH, YOU'RE *TWO* DOCTORS

The Jeremy Clarkson lectures

FRESH FROM RECEIVING NOT ONE, BUT TWO DOCTORATES IN THE POST, DOCTOR DOCTOR JEREMY CLARKSON WAS INVITED TO MAKE A KEYNOTE SPEECH TO THE BRITISH INSTITUTE OF BOFFINS & BOFFINERY. HERE IS AN EXACT TRANSCRIPT OF THAT LANDMARK ADDRESS

Hello and welcome. And I'm going to start tonight with a question: what is gravity? Well, I think the answer is that it's a load of nonsense. Think about it. If the Earth is spinning round, why aren't we all flung off into space? Yet in fact, we're stuck to the Earth's surface. Plainly this is wrong, so don't come crying to me when you find yourself suddenly having to cling to a heavy object to stop yourself flying off into the sky.

Now, as I've just proved, gravity is basically rubbish and does not exist. But what about the principles of flight? Well, as you'd expect, I've researched these thoroughly. I did this by speaking to James May, and after less than three minutes I found myself literally losing the will to live. From this we can deduce that flight is essentially so boring, no one can understand it, and it is my conclusion that the very second anyone actually does understand flight, all planes will fall out of the sky.

Why are you leaving? And you. Come back here. I haven't finished yet.

I want to talk next about a question I'm often asked: what is torque? Well, obviously torque is something that's far too tedious to waste your time

trying to understand. The best way to explain it is to think of an elephant. Have you got that? Good. You've just thought of something more interesting than torque. Fact!

Right, you can stop thinking of the elephant now. And stop moving slowly towards the exits. I've got lots more to get through.

Now, being two doctors means I have lots of doctoring power to spare and recently I've been using it to consider the difficult question of the economy. Specifically, where did it all go wrong? Well, it's quite simple. All of the banks in the world lent eleventy squillion dollars to a man in Mexico who wanted to build an extension on his house, but they forgot to ask if the man in Mexico could repay the loan, which of course he couldn't, as a result of which all the banks ran out of money and that is precisely why a lazy man in Mexico is responsible for all the shops on the high street being shut.

Why are you booing?

Now I'd like to turn my attention to what is wrong with the Greeks...

STOP THROWING THINGS AT ME

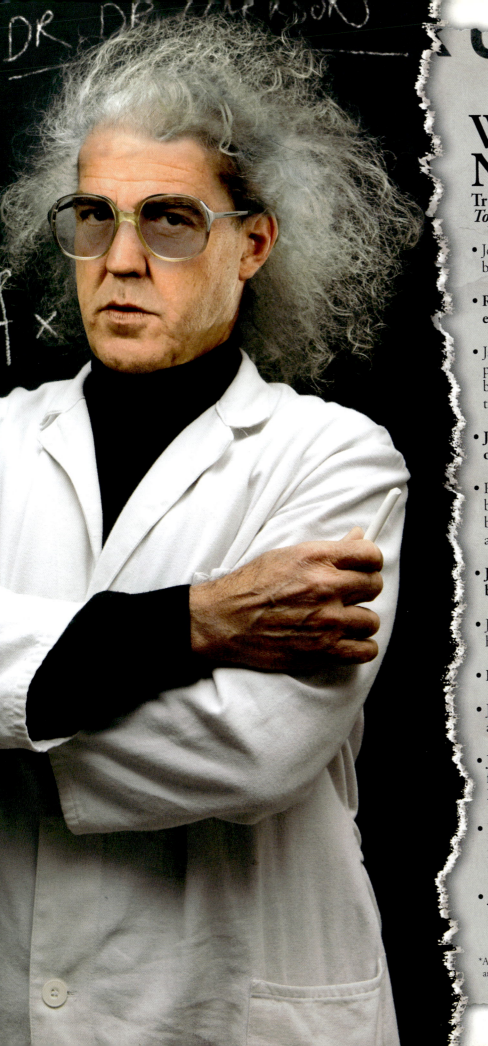

WELL I NEVER!
True facts about the _Top Gear_ presenters*

- Jeremy is quite interested in birdwatching.

- **Richard is good at sketching, especially cars.**

- James is the only _Top Gear_ presenter who could kick a ball and watch it travel in the direction he intended.

- **Jeremy is almost three years older than James.**

- Richard likes running, bicycling and horse riding, but is surprisingly rubbish at playing snooker.

- **James only bought his house because it had a garage.**

- Jeremy has a pathological hatred of short-sleeved shirts.

- **Richard owns a set of bongos.**

- James has a set of nail clippers attached to his keys.

- **Jeremy thinks the greatest film ever made is Bill Forsyth's _Local Hero_.**

- Richard's idea of a good holiday is walking in the Lake District.

- **James and Jeremy own the same sort of watch. It's an Omega Railmaster.**

*And unlike most things in this book, these really are true. Which is why they're not that interesting.

What's My Job? – I Manufacture Weaklings into MEN!

James May

Warning: actual James May may not match photograph.

Oh, hullo. In this modern age of jet aeroplanes and portable gramophones it can be rather tricky to maintain your weight, what with all that running around the Internet and listening to the latest beat combos and such like. But don't worry, with the **JAMES MAY DIET PLAN** you can be sure to stay at your target weight, whatever the world throws at you!

STEAK + KIDNEY   PORK PIE   APPLE CRUMBLE

How does it work?

Here's a typical day on the JAMES MAY DIET PLAN

BREAKFAST: Beef Hula Hoops, cup o' tea

MID-MORNING SNACK: Beef Hula Hoops, handful of American Hard Gums, cup o' tea

LUNCH: Cheese & onion pie, bag of beef Hula Hoops, can of ginger beer, iced bun, cup o' tea

MID-AFTERNOON SNACK: Half a steak & kidney pie, cup o' tea

LATE-AFTERNOON SNACK: Other half of the steak & kidney pie, cup o' tea

DINNER: Chicken & bacon pie, chips, peas, can of ginger beer, apple crumble and custard, cup o' tea

SUPPER: Pork pie (small), bag of plain Hula Hoops (shop had run out of beef ones), cup o' tea

But that sounds dangerously unhealthy!

Yes, by following a hearty, heavy and slightly flatulent menu such as this, you too can maintain the stout figure of a middle-aged man who lives on his own and likes old motorcycles – today!

THE JAMES MAY DIET PLAN
Putting the 'pie' in 'diet'

WARNING: may cause chest pains and faecal urgency.

FREE

The **JAMES MAY DIET PLAN** is designed to offer YOU all the steak, kidney, cheese and onion that your body needs, plus 1200 per cent of your daily recommended intake of tea. And crisps.

PIES

THE JAMES MAY DIET PLAN,
PO Box 43, London.

I want proof that your system of **massive pastry consumption** will help make a new man of me, giving me a healthy body and extremely luxuriant hair. Please send me your free book, *Pies Before Bedtime.*

Name ....

Address ....

Trousers ....

THE ZANY WORLD OF DR. CLARKSON

RIGHT, THAT'S THE V8 HOOKED UP TO THE PENCIL SHARPENER.

I SHALL CALL UPON MY FAITHFUL ASSISTANT GAVIN TO HELP ME WITH THE TEST RUN. GAVIN!

RIGHT, SIMPLY INSERT THE PENCIL INTO THE PENCIL HOLE AND I'LL FIRE HER UP.

WHIIIRRRRSPLATT!!!

THAT'S STRANGE. GAVIN APPEARS TO HAVE BECOME HORRIFICALLY INJURED.

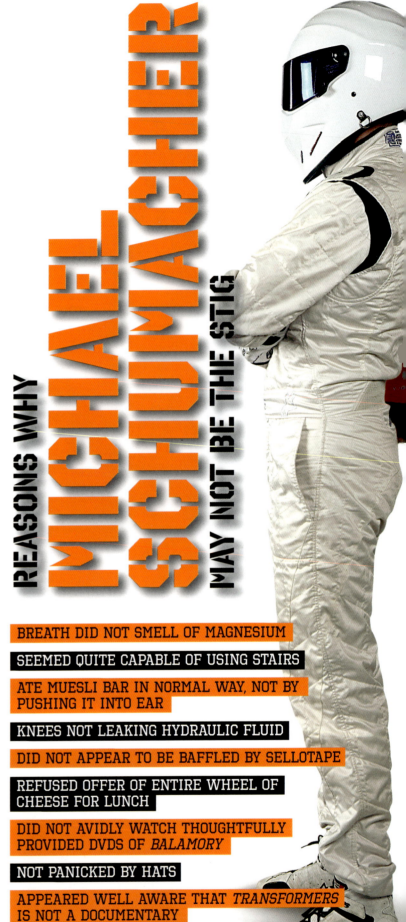

REASONS WHY MICHAEL SCHUMACHER MAY NOT BE THE STIG

BREATH DID NOT SMELL OF MAGNESIUM

SEEMED QUITE CAPABLE OF USING STAIRS

ATE MUESLI BAR IN NORMAL WAY, NOT BY PUSHING IT INTO EAR

KNEES NOT LEAKING HYDRAULIC FLUID

DID NOT APPEAR TO BE BAFFLED BY SELLOTAPE

REFUSED OFFER OF ENTIRE WHEEL OF CHEESE FOR LUNCH

DID NOT AVIDLY WATCH THOUGHTFULLY PROVIDED DVDS OF *BALAMORY*

NOT PANICKED BY HATS

APPEARED WELL AWARE THAT *TRANSFORMERS* IS NOT A DOCUMENTARY

ANOTHER STIG FOUND TIED TO A CHAIR. MIND YOU, THAT HAPPENS A LOT.

geek zone

1

Wow your friends and impress the ladies with these amazing car facts

01 The Ferrari FXX lapped around the track in series 13 of *Top Gear* actually belonged to Michael Stigmacher and is chassis number 30, the very last car made. Ferrari intended to build just 29 FXXs but when the bloke who's scored you six F1 constructors' titles decides he'd like one too, you're not going to say no.

02 **During development of the Jaguar XFR, the engineers working on the car unofficially codenamed it 'Weapon of Choice'.**

03 The distinctive, black, rear pillars on all generations of Range Rover are actually derived from bodgery on the original 1970 model. Shortly before it went on sale, someone at the factory noticed that the aluminium skin on the rear pillars looked rippled, and therefore a bit rubbish. Since it was impossible to get rid of the ripples they simply covered them with a piece of black vinyl, thereby accidentally giving birth to a design feature that continues on Range Rovers to this day.

04 Back when Vauxhall used to design complete cars in Britain, it had a styling studio in Luton with an outside viewing yard so that management could look at the full-size models of forthcoming new cars under natural light. Then, one day, someone noticed a new block of flats was being built next door and that the residents of the top-floor properties would be able to see straight into the viewing yard, giving them a great vantage point from which to take pictures of top-secret new designs and sell them to the highest bidder. So when the building was finished, Vauxhall simply bought all the flats that overlooked their land and left them empty. Some years later the Vauxhall design studio closed down, the upside of which was that they were then able to sell the flats and make a tidy profit in the process.

---

myface   Home   Profile   Friends   Inbox

 Richard Hammond is the BLACK SHADOW. Dun-dun-dun-dun-dun-dudderdun-dun-durrrrrrr.
4 hours ago · Comment · Like

myface   Home   Profile   Friends   Inbox

 Richard Hammond does NOT live in Wales.
50 minutes ago ·

myface   Home   Profile   Friends   Inbox

 Richard Hammond is going to the dentist. Don't say it Clarkson. I know you're thinking it. It's not for that. It's NOT. If I get back and there's a message from you saying it's for that I'm going to come round and insert sharp things into your head and torso.
7 minutes ago · Comment · Like

UNIVERSITY OF TOP GEAR
(FORMERLY WHEELBASE POLYTECHNIC)

RESEARCH QUESTIONNAIRE

Research scientist: Dr Dr Clarkson
Research hypothesis: Richard Hammond's house is not in England
Aim of questionnaire: To prove that Hammond lives in Wales

Question 1
Do you like lamb?

☐ Yes ☐ Yes

Question 2
Do you enjoy close-harmony singing?

☐ Yes ☐ Yes

Question 3
Do all your words have the letter L in them at least seven times?

☐ Yes ☐ Yes

Question 4
When you talk to someone, do you continually drench them in phlegm?

☐ Yes ☐ Yes

Question 5
Do you find this woman attractive?

☐ Yes ☐ Yes

Question 6
Do you find this man attractive?

☐ Yes ☐ Yes

Question 7
Do you find this animal attractive?

☐ Yes ☐ Yes

Question 8
Do you live in Wales?

☐ Yes ☐ Yes

Research conclusion:
Hammond is Welsh. Fact.

Bigglesmay

THE GENTLEMAN FLYER

in *JERRY WORE WHITE*

LORD "JEREMY" CLARKSON SCANNED THE FLAT AIRFIELD IN FRONT OF HIM, ITS RUNWAYS AND TAXIWAYS BATHED IN THE SUNLIGHT OF A PERFECT ENGLISH SUMMER'S DAY, EASED BACK IN HIS FOLDAWAY WOODEN CHAIR AND LET OUT A LONG EXHALATION.

DASH IT ALL HAMSTER, I'M BORED,

HE HUFFED.

THE PERSON TO WHOM THIS REMARK WAS ADDRESSED, CLARKSON'S FRIEND AND COLLEAGUE RICHARD "HAMSTER" HAMMOND, BARELY ACKNOWLEDGED IT, ENGROSSED AS HE WAS IN THE LATEST CATALOGUE FROM THE MORGAN MOTOR COMPANY.

CLARKSON REPEATED WITH MORE EMPHASIS, DRUMMING HIS HANDS ON THE WOODEN TABLE THAT THE TWO CHUMS HAD CAREFULLY POSITIONED ON THE GRASS BEHIND THE OLD FLIGHT OPS SHED SO THAT THEY COULD BEST ENJOY THIS PERIOD OF INACTIVITY REVELLING IN THE GLORIOUS WEATHER.

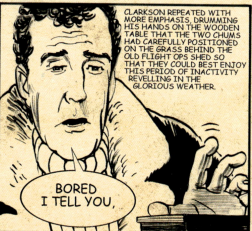

BORED I TELL YOU,

HAMMOND CONTINUED TO IGNORE HIS OLDER, BALDER, COMRADE AS THE IDLE INVECTIVE SHOWED NO SIGNS OF ABATING.

BORED, BORED, BORED, BORED, BORED... IS THERE SOMETHING I COULD HIT WITH A HAMMER? THAT WOULD CHEER ME UP.

AT THIS MOMENT A FAMILIAR, SHAGGY-HAIRED FIGURE CAME STALKING ACROSS THE GRASS TOWARDS THEM.

OH LORD,

CLARKSON MUTTERED, SOTTO VOCE.

THIS IS GOING TO DO NOTHING FOR MY BOREDOM.

THE LAST OF LORD JEREMY'S JOCULAR WORDS HAD JUST LEFT HIS MOUTH BEFORE THE ADVANCING FIGURE WAS TOWERING ABOVE THE SMALL FOLDAWAY TABLE, A NOBLE SILHOUETTE AGAINST THE SUN, HIS FLOWING LOCKS BLOWING IN THE GENTLE BREEZE THAT EBBED AND FLOWED ACROSS THE SURREY COUNTRYSIDE. CLARKSON AND HAMMOND BOTH TURNED SLIGHTLY AND GAVE BRIEF BUT RESPECTFUL ACKNOWLEDGMENT: CAPTAIN JAMES BIGGLESMAY STOOD BEFORE THEM.

HULLO CHAPS,

ALL AT ONCE HIS RUGGED BROW CRINKLED AND CREASED WITH AN OBVIOUS CONCERN THAT PLAYED ON HIS KEEN AND FEARSOME MIND.

NOW I DON'T WANT TO WORRY YOU CHAPS, BUT THERE'S SOMETHING BALLY QUEER GOING ON WITH OLD STIGGY...

HAMMOND'S EYES BARELY FLICKERED UP FROM HIS READING MATERIAL WHILST CLARKSON SINGULARLY FAILED TO FEIGN AN INTEREST. BIGGLESMAY CONTINUED NONE THE LESS;

I WENT TO GIVE HIM HIS CUSTOMARY AFTERNOON SNACK AND HE JUST WASN'T BLOOMING INTERESTED, NOT IN THE RAW POTATO, NOT IN THE POUND OF LARD....

MAYBE HE'S JUST NOT HUNGRY,

MURMURED HAMMOND WITHOUT SHIFTING HIS GAZE FROM THE SPORTS CARS ON THE PAGE IN FRONT OF HIM.

WELL THAT'S WHAT I THOUGHT, SO I WENT TO EMERGENCY MEASURES...

DEFCON 1

CHIMED CLARKSON, SUDDENLY SHOWING WHAT MIGHT ALMOST PASS FOR ENTHUSIASM.

HAMMOND ROLLED HIS EYES.

I DON'T THINK THAT PHRASE HAS BEEN INVENTED YET,

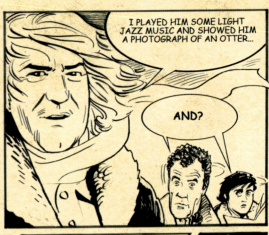

I PLAYED HIM SOME LIGHT JAZZ MUSIC AND SHOWED HIM A PHOTOGRAPH OF AN OTTER...

AND?

NOTHING

THE MORGAN BROCHURE FLEW IN THE AIR, ALONG WITH CLARKSON'S CUP OF TEA AS THE TWO BRAVE FLYERS LEAPT FROM THEIR FLIMSY WOODEN CHAIRS SIMULTANEOUSLY EXCLAIMING A FEARFUL...

WHAT??

BUT THOSE ARE THE TWO THINGS GUARANTEED TO DRIVE STIGGY INTO A FURY! AND YOU'RE SAYING HE DID NOTHING?

SOMETHING IS VERY WRONG, WHERE IS HE NOW?

WITH THE SAME CALM ATTITUDE THAT HAS SEEN HIM THROUGH COUNTLESS CRISES, BIGGLESMAY LEAD HIS TWO CHUMS INTO THE FLIGHT OPS SHED AND CAUTIOUSLY OPENED THE DOOR TO THE STIG'S CHAMBER. WHAT GREETED HIS EYES WAS YET ANOTHER SHOCK:

FLIGHT OPS

CLARKSON SCANNED THE MAIN OPS ROOM BEHIND HIM;

AND LOOK, ALL THE TOP SECRET PLANS HAVE GONE. AND THE SPECIAL CODE MACHINE!

PLANS

CODE MACHINE

DASH IT ALL! HE'S BALLY WELL GONE!

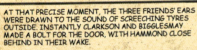

AT THAT PRECISE MOMENT, THE THREE FRIENDS' EARS WERE DRAWN TO THE SOUND OF SCREECHING TYRES OUTSIDE. INSTANTLY CLARKSON AND BIGGLESMAY MADE A BOLT FOR THE DOOR, WITH HAMMOND CLOSE BEHIND IN THEIR WAKE.

SCREECH!!!

AS THEY REACHED THE DOOR OUT OF THE OPS SHED THEY COULD SCARCELY BELIEVE WHAT THEY SAW.

STIG!

THE PAIR SHOUTED IN UNISON AS THEIR BRAVE COMRADE IN WHITE SPED AWAY IN A LIGHT BLUE CHEVROLET LACETTI.

FLIGHT OPS

KRAU

HIDDEN BEHIND THE LONG GRASS AT THE VERY FURTHEST EXTREME OF THE OLD AIRFIELD WAS STIG'S DESTINATION:

A PRIVATE JET!

OH...WHAT? COME ON, THESE HAVEN'T BEEN BLOODY INVENTED YET. THIS STORY IS BECOMING EXTREMELY UNREALIST...

HE'S GOING TO GET AWAY!

DASH IT ALL, WE HAVE TO STOP HIM. DRIVE HAMMOND, DRIVE!

THE BOYISH AIR ACE PLUNGED THE ACCELERATOR PEDAL OF HIS BELOVED SPORTS CAR AND BROUGHT IT SCREECHING ALONGSIDE THE SLEEK AND FUTURISTIC GULFSTREAM

NOT SO FAST STIGGY!

STIGGY?

ZAT IS NOT MEINE REAL NAME...

MICHAEL SCHUMACHER !?

GUTBYE MEINE BRITISCHE CHUMS. HA HA HA!

AND WITH THAT HE LEAPT INTO HIS **IMPOSSIBLY FUTURISTIC JET** AND BEGAN TO TAXI TOWARDS THE RUNWAY.

THE PERFIDIOUS JERRY IS MAKING A RUN FOR IT!

DON'T WORRY CHAPS, WE'LL CATCH HIM. MY OLD KITE'S JUST OVER HERE...

QUICK! LET'S GET GOING!

AND WITH THAT, BIGGLESMAY SWEPT ASIDE SOME BUSHES AND, TO THE DELIGHT OF HIS TWO FRIENDS, REVEALED HIS OLD **SUPER DECATHLON** PARKED NOT 10 FEET AWAY.

SUPER DECATHLON? AREN'T WE, LIKE, 25 YEARS TOO EARLY FOR ONE OF THOSE...

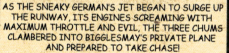

AS THE SNEAKY GERMAN'S JET BEGAN TO SURGE UP THE RUNWAY, ITS ENGINES SCREAMING WITH MAXIMUM THROTTLE AND EVIL, THE THREE CHUMS CLAMBERED INTO BIGGLESMAY'S PRIVATE PLANE AND PREPARED TO TAKE CHASE!

RIGHT, FIRST I NEED TO CHECK THE FUEL...

WHAT? JUST GO! GO JAMES GO!

IF THERE'S ANY CONDENSATION GOT INTO THE TANKS THAT'LL NEED TO BE TAKEN CARE OF...

...NOW I NEED TO RUN THROUGH THE RUDDER FUNCTION TEST. IT'S VERY QUICK AND SHOULD TAKE NO MORE THAN 45 MINUTES...

OH GOD...

HE'S GETTING AWAY!

...THEN OF COURSE THERE'S THE FULL CHECK OF ALL FLAPS AND AILERON FUNCTIONS AND RELATED SYSTEMS...

FOR THE LOVE OF GOD...!

...NOW ONCE THAT'S DONE OF COURSE I NEED TO FULLY CHART OUR PROPOSED ROUTE AND RADIO ALL RELEVANT AIR TRAFFIC CONTROL NODES ALONG THAT ROUTE TO INFORM THEM OF OUR TRAJECTORY AND IN TURN RECEIVE INFORMATION ABOUT OTHER AIRCRAFT THAT MAY BE IN OUR AREA AT THE TIME...

sob

sigh

MY JOB

NICKI CILLITBANG HAS BEEN THE COSTUME DESIGNER FOR THE BBC SHOW *TOP GEAR* SINCE 2002. HE TALKS ABOUT THE CHALLENGES OF DRESSING ITS THREE PRESENTERS

i REMEMBER THE DAY, SEVEN YEARS AGO, WHEN THE BBC CALLED to say it was bringing back *Top Gear* and asked me to be the costume designer. I admit I had concerns, and these were made worse when I met Jeremy Clarkson for the first time. This tall, lean man walked in, immaculately dressed in a black Armani suit with a crisp black shirt underneath, and I thought, 'Well, this is going to be a challenge!' Whenever I'm designing costumes I start with some key phrases that sum up the character. In Jeremy's case these were 'middle-aged', 'geography teacher' and 'buys clothes by running into a shop with his eyes closed and grabbing things that are near the door'. The real starting point was the paunch. I got hold of a fake pregnancy tummy from *EastEnders*, and Jeremy agreed to try it on. Of course it was perfect, and even under his neatly pressed Hugo Boss shirt it immediately gave him the appearance of a man who just sits around drinking coffee and smoking cigarettes! With that in place, I started scouring second-hand shops for battered jeans, smart-casual jackets and the kind of shirts your dad might wear when he thought he was being 'cool'. It took a while to coax Jeremy out of his Gaultier and Galliano, but even he eventually agreed that we had found a look to suit the character. Only the perm caused a real argument and I'm pleased to say I won that one!

My next challenge was Richard Hammond. The first few times I met him he arrived from the countryside in his regular uniform of dungarees and a stained white T-shirt, neither of which worked for me, character-wise. I had been studying the look of several boy bands and suggested that we go for something similar. Richard took to my ideas in an instant, especially the one about wearing shoes 'not just on special occasions'. My biggest triumph was introducing him to hair gel. Once he'd tried it for the first time he just couldn't get enough of it! I ended up having to hide the jar!

Top Gear returned to our screens with great success and I was extremely proud of my costume designs. For series two, however, the producers really threw me a curve ball when they announced that they were bringing in a chap called James May. Now here was a flamboyant character, with his open shirts, leather trousers and his many necklaces and bracelets. In many ways he put me in mind of a young Jim Morrison, something that didn't really sit with the character he would be playing on *Top Gear*. I started researching his look by visiting a classic car show and observing the rather strange, single men in the crowd. It was all the inspiration I needed and, though I stopped short of giving James a beard, I did persuade him to let me remodel his gorgeous, slicked back hair into a new style that was based on a photograph of a spaniel I found in a book. The real breakthrough, clothes-wise, was when I found a stripy jumper in a skip near my house. At one point I thought James should simply wear this every week! Sadly, I feared this would add even more holes and stains to it until it became unusable, so I've restricted it to just one appearance every two shows. With the hair, the oil stained jeans and of course another strap-on pregnancy paunch – thanks props department at *Holby City*! – James's look was complete. No one would ever recognize the snake-hipped and showy man of yore now that I had transformed him into the bloke who props up the bar in your local pub, doing the crossword and grumbling about his 1970s motorcycle!

Seven years on, I'm always tweaking and evolving the *Top Gear* boys' looks – a bigger paunch and a dab of grey hair dye for Jeremy; a shaggy wig and D'Artagnan-meets-Spandau Ballet clothes for Richard; hair modelled on a different spaniel and a new stripy jumper found in a canal for James – but I'm delighted to say that the basic looks I set out still work to this day!

'IT TOOK A WHILE TO COAX JEREMY OUT OF HIS GAULTIER!'

GREAT NAMES

IF YOU WANT TO GET ON IN THE WORLD OF CARS, YOU NEED A GOOD NAME, AS THE FOLLOWING PEOPLE PROVE...

Victor Gauntlett

Former owner of Aston Martin. With a name like that, he was BORN to do it.

Jenson Button

First name inspired by a car, last name an absolute GIFT for tabloid headline writers.

Scott Speed

American racing driver. Gloss over how crap he was in F1, at least he SOUNDS fast.

Max Venturi

Lamborghini test driver. Bet they gave him a job and THEN bothered to ask if he could actually drive.

Martin Peach

Once Rover's head of – wait for it – colour and trim. Could never have been head of IT SYSTEMS.

On the other hand...

THIS LOT SEEMED TO MANAGE DESPITE THEIR NAMES, NOT BECAUSE OF THEM...

NIGEL MANSELL

Bulldog determination and race-winning pace are all well and good, but honestly, is NIGEL really the name for an F1 world champion?

BRUNO SACCO

Italian gentleman responsible for a myriad great-looking Mercedes throughout the '70s, '80s and '90s. All of which is undermined because in his homeland his name means 'BROWN BAG'.

KEN OKUYAMA

As a car designer, he's created Corvettes and Porsches and, during his time at Pininfarina, the Ferrari Enzo and 599. But he's called Ken. It's not COOL is it?

KNUT SIMONSSON

Currently SAAB's Executive Director for Global Brand & Sales Operations whilst simultaneously acting as a one-man, typing-error MINEFIELD.

THE BEAULIEU MOTOR MUSEUM

A fine day out, marred only because it is literally impossible to spell. Even this might not be correct. NO ONE KNOWS.

BBC

TOP GEAR
RISK ASSESSMENT FORM

Version 2

Form: 27268/beaura/457dr/ cratic/903ev/nons/23Lvs/ense

Programme	*TOP GEAR*	Series	Series 14
Production address	*Top Gear* Production Office 201 Wood Lane London W12 7TN	Producer/Editor	
Date		Version Number	

Assessor	Name Signature	Date completed	
Authorized by (if not Assessor)	Name Signature	Date authorized	

A: Hazard list – *select your hazard from the list below and use these to complete section B*

General Hazards	Tick	General Hazards	Tick	Stig-Specific Hazards	Tick
Attack by person		Risk of piano falling on Morris Marina		Given Maltesers	
Attack by animal		Risk of attack by Morris Marina Owners' Club		Shown picture of Moira Stewart	
Attack by Richard Hammond		Wry eyebrows		Realizes he's in Ipswich	
Attack of flatulence (James May only)		Unsupervised smirking		Hydraulic fluid loss (legs)	
Jeremy has got hold of a hammer		Large dog in small car		Hydraulic fluid loss (head)	
Shot at by British Army (again)		Honey badgers		Confused by stairs	
Shouting 'Poweeeeer!' in loud voice		Other badgers		Near owls	
Massive power slides		Someone shouting 'Watch this!'		Tries to understand scissors	
Becoming tangled in large analogy		Entire car cost £207		Told about death of Michael Jackson	
Inappropriate use of the word 'literally'		Deliberately crashing into things		Within 20 metres of Scouts	
James May explanation going on so long everybody wants to kill themselves		Accidental exposure to the contents of Jeremy Clarkson's iPod		Nigel Havers	

B: Risk matrix – *use to determine risk for each hazard; i.e. 'how bad and how likely?'*

Severity of harm	Likelihood of harm				
	Remote *<1 in 1000 chance*	**Unlikely** *1 in 200 chance*	**Possible** *1 in 50 chance*	**Likely** *1 in 10 chance*	**Probable** *1 in 3 chance*
Negligible *e.g. Oh God, we're sinking*	Very low	Very low	Very low	Low	Low
Slight *e.g. Ouch! That smarts a bit*	Very low	Very low	Low	Low	Medium
Moderate *e.g. Yes, I am definitely on fire now*	Very low	Low	Medium	Medium	High
Severe *e.g. Would you like your hand back?*	Low	Medium	Medium	High	Extremely high
Very severe *e.g. Anyway, if you'd like to present Top Gear why not write to us...*	Low	Medium	High	Extremely high	Oh SHIT!

FORD FIESTA
THE REJECTED TESTS

When Jeremy set out to conduct a 'thorough' road test of the latest Ford Fiesta, he really was very, very thorough indeed, answering important questions such as 'What happens if you go to a shopping centre and get chased by some baddies in a Corvette?' and 'What if you're asked to take part in a beach assault with the Royal Marines?' There were, however, some key tests that, although vital to any comprehensive analysis of a new small car, did not make it into Clarkson's report. Here, for the first time, we can list the rejected ones in full.

Is it resistant to attack from giant futuristic robot wasps?

Does the actor Nigel Havers like it?

What does it taste like?

RAAR

Can you drive it whilst dressed in a lion costume?

What is Archbishop Desmond Tutu's favourite bit of the dashboard?

The Glovebox

Were any parts of the engine designed by a man called Sven?

Is it possible to surprise a Canadian in it?

In an emergency, could you swap it for some horses?

Neigh!

What happens if you feed slices of meat into the CD player?

Where would be the best place to hide cheeses?

FRENCHY PONG

AUDI QUATTRO

Some of the most legendary cars come about when companies get a bit Dr Frankenstein, melding together bits they've found in their workshops in an unholy manner. And so it was with the famous Audi Quattro.

The coupé shell existed – it was going to be a new, mildly sporty version of the upcoming Audi 80 saloon – and the four-wheel-drive mechanics were there – but they were created for a small jeep that VW was developing for the military. All it needed was for a select team of excitable Audi engineers to have the radical idea of bringing them together.

At the time, four-wheel drive was seen as something rough and crude that was only necessary on off-road vehicles. To persuade Audi bosses that it could be used to make sports coupés better, the engineers brought the management bods to the slippery roads of the Alps and let them loose in the prototype. They gave it the go-ahead for production in an instant.

And so a road and rallying legend was born. Not the first four-wheel-drive sports car ever, but the first to make it actually work. And work well.

Top Gear

As *Top Gear* has become more popular, it's not just the programme itself that is sold to other TV channels around the world...

Now, the basic format of the show is being flogged abroad so that Mr Jonathan Foreigner can make his own version of the world's most popular programme that is loosely about cars, but mostly about things falling over and then catching fire. However, whilst the fundamentals of any overseas version of *Top Gear* are the same, there are of course tweaks to make it more palatable and comprehensible to a local audience. Here, for example, are some of the changes made for the new Austrian version of *Top Gear*, presented by Johann Clarksöhn, Reinhard Hammönd and Jürgen May.

Johann

Reinhard

Jürgen

Around The World

How hard can it be?	We performed a thorough analysis of the problems inherent in this task and decided that it was not feasible.
Jeremy was the first to arrive.	We all arrived together, at precisely the agreed time.
Ha ha, Richard you are small!	I have observed, Reinhard, that there is precisely 9.8cm difference between our respective heights and this amuses me.
Oh no, here comes Captain Slow!	Oh no, here comes Captain On-Average-5.6kph-Below-The-Prevailing-Speed-Limit. I should add that he is not technically a Captain since he holds no senior position within either aviation or shipping.
That's not gone well...	This has been achieved with technical precision, as usual.
Ah James, got lost again, did we?	Ah Jürgen, follow the directions and arrive at the allotted meeting place with no problems, did we?
We were ambitious, but rubbish.	We had realistic goals, and they were fully achieved.
And on that bombshell, it's time to say goodnight!	And having presented to you a series of events we have reached the end of our prescribed time. Commensurately, the transmission will now end.

Und now, a star in a relatively affordable vehicle

THE ZANY WORLD OF DR. CLARKSON

YES, THIS SHOULD GET THE CARPETS CLEAN IN RECORD TIME...

...ESPECIALLY WITH THIS HANDY V8 ON IT. NOW TO TEST IT. GAVIN! AWAY YOU GO...

VVVRRRRRRR!!!!!

THAT'S STRANGE. GAVIN APPEARS TO HAVE BECOME HORRIFICALLY INJURED.

AGAIN.

geek zone

Become 403 per cent more interesting with these brilliant car facts

01 Peugeot is best known for making cars and, to a slightly lesser degree, bicycles. But the company has owned a range of businesses over the years including a kitchen-appliance company, which in the 1960s announced a brand-new food processor called the Peugimix.

02 Ford's Edsel project still ranks as one of the biggest disasters in car history, chiefly because the American auto giant spent a fortune coming up with a whole family of goppingly ugly cars and then was puzzled when they were a sales disaster. These desperate times called for desperate measures, one of which was to give each Edsel dealer a real, live pony. On paper this was a genius plan. Kids would pester their parents to let them go to look at the little horsey, and once in there the smooth salesman would work on dad until he bought a car. Sadly, the scheme overlooked three major problems. First of all, the typical car dealer isn't really trained to look after a pony. Secondly, the kids may have been happy petting the animal, but did dad really want to buy a new car from a place that stank of horse poo? And finally, once the promotion was over, what was Ford going to do with hundreds of unwanted ponies? Best not to think too hard about that one. Suffice to say, they probably didn't need to buy any glue for a while.

03 During the 2002 US GP, Jaguar driver Pedro de la Rosa broke down on the far side of the track, got out of his car and jumped over a low wall without checking what was on the other side. Unfortunately, it was a river. He thereby became the only F1 driver ever to fall into a free flowing body of water DURING a race.

myface Home Profile Friends Inbox

James May doesn't understand how this YouBook thing works.

myface Home Profile Friends Inbox

James May has discovered that you are meant to write what you're doing in this little box. James May is currently typing in this little box.

16 minutes ago • Comment • Like

Gazump&Gazunda

'WHITE TOWERS'
£120,000,000.00

A rare opportunity to acquire the desirable country residence of *Top Gear*'s tame racing driver. Some say this property is located within easy reach of Silverstone, Brands Hatch, the Nürburgring and Spa-Francorchamps. 'White Towers' boasts ample parking as well as a bright, airy interior, some of which doesn't smell too strongly of hot pork and photo-processing chemicals.

It is very rare for properties of this calibre to come up for sale, especially ones with an *en suite* trouser press in every room and a family of furious otters living in the floor cavities. As such, viewing is highly recommended at your earliest convenience. However, as the current owner is sometimes quite unpleasant, we would ask for your patience as viewings are only advisable when he is out, especially since no one wants a repeat of what happened last week, least of all the local Scout troop.

VOTED 'MOST DUPLICITOUS GITS' – **PROPERTY AWARDS 2009**

Gazump&Gazunda

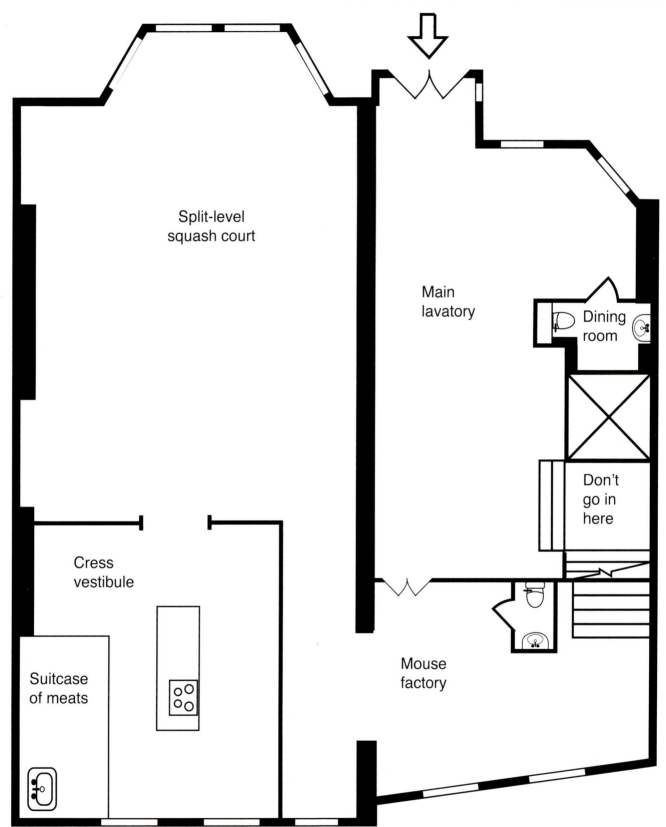

Split-level
squash court

Main
lavatory

Dining
room

Don't
go in
here

Cress
vestibule

Suitcase
of meats

Mouse
factory

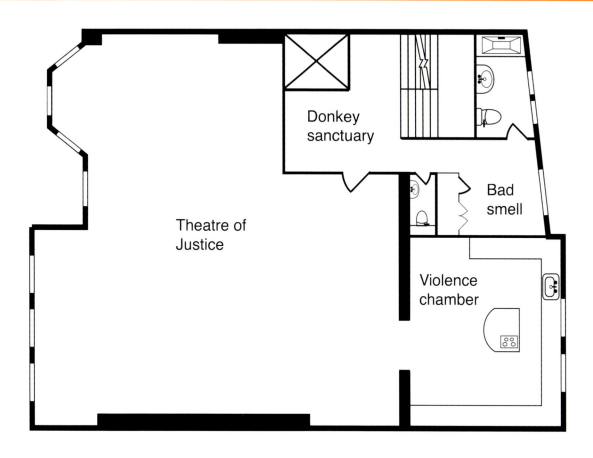

Donkey sanctuary

Bad smell

Theatre of Justice

Violence chamber

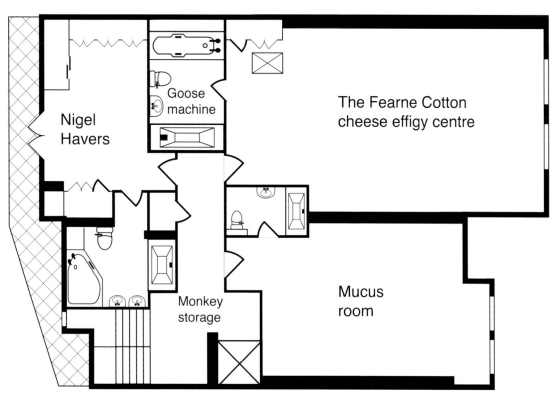

Nigel Havers

Goose machine

The Fearne Cotton cheese effigy centre

Monkey storage

Mucus room

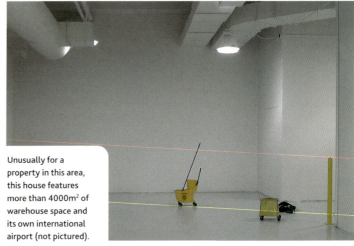

Words alone cannot do justice to the rare desirability, unusual fragrance and frankly baffling layout of this remarkable property. To appreciate all of its qualities in full, you would need to hover 44 feet above it in a hot air balloon operated by the actor, singer and irritant John Barrowman. If this is not possible, we would nonetheless recommend a lengthy viewing in order that you might appraise fully this property's unique features, including its ample inspection pits, well-stocked hat shop and deeply upsetting downstairs lavatory. Houses as stylish and as overrun with strange things as this very rarely come on the market and, as you are no doubt aware, many are never advertised since they are immediately snapped up by Nigel Havers.

Naturally, this house features a frankly inexplicable number of showers. Ideal for anyone who habitually needs to rinse off the evidence again.

Unusually for a property in this area, this house features more than 4000m² of warehouse space and its own international airport (not pictured).

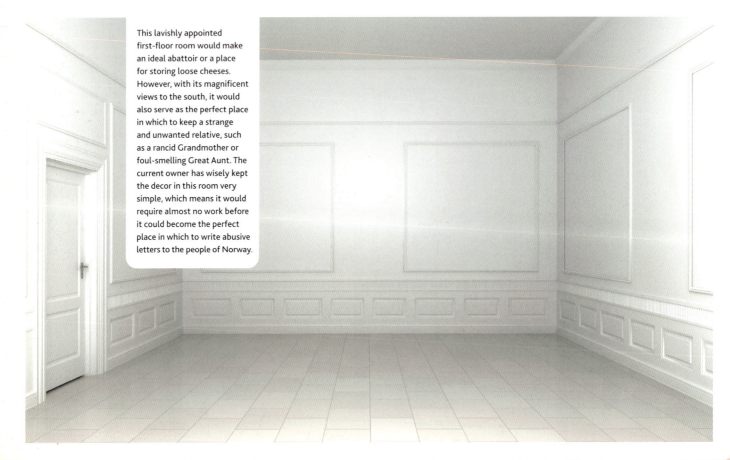

This lavishly appointed first-floor room would make an ideal abattoir or a place for storing loose cheeses. However, with its magnificent views to the south, it would also serve as the perfect place in which to keep a strange and unwanted relative, such as a rancid Grandmother or foul-smelling Great Aunt. The current owner has wisely kept the decor in this room very simple, which means it would require almost no work before it could become the perfect place in which to write abusive letters to the people of Norway.

HAMMOND'S

VIETNAMESE RESTAURANT

WHERE EAST MEETS WEST MIDLANDS

Hu Tieu Thap Cam 属 記憶
Smells of fish.

Tam Bi Cha 属 記憶 金
*No idea what this is.
It's got bits in it.*

Tom Rim Cha 属 記憶
*Are those shrimps? Errrr.
Don't like fish.*

Ga Xao Xa Ot 属 記
*Smells a bit like washing-
up liquid. Nasty.*

Bo Kho 属 記憶 金属 記憶 金
*This looks a bit like stew.
Bet it isn't though.
Not with this lot.*

**Bun Bo Hue Gio Cha
Gan Huyet** 属 記憶 金属 記
*Sort of soupy stuff with
gristle floating in it.
Thanks, but no thanks.*

Banh Canh Gio Heo 属 記
*Bloody hell, is that
a foot? I'm definitely
not eating that.*

Com Xao Chay 属 記
*Ah, now this is rice. But rice
with bits in it. Ruined.*

記憶 **Mi Tom Cua**
Really smells of fish.

属 記憶 **Tam Bo Nuong**
*Don't like the look of this.
Think it's got pork in.
Or beef. Either way, not
eating it.*

憶 **Tam Tau Hu Ky**
*Is this meant to look like
that? It's got skin in it. Yuck.*

記憶 **Vit Quay**
*Sort of greasy thing with
stuff on it. No ta.*

Tau Hu Ky Doi Cha
記憶 **Suon Nuong**
*That's not a finger is it? It
better not be a finger. It is.
It's a… no, surely not.*

記憶 金属 記憶 **Bun Rieu**
*Don't know where to start
with this one. Bet you can't
get chips with it.*

記憶 **Chao Huyet**
*Oh my God, is that blood?
I feel sick.*

**ALL ORDERS OVER £10
RECEIVE FREE BAG OF VILE-
SMELLING BROWN MUSH!**

The TopGear Magnetic Amphibious Vehicle Fishing Game

All the fun of haphazard aquatic adventures in your very own living room! Recreate the boys' doomed voyage to France using your big magnetic rod to avoid ending up in Stiggy-Jones' locker

The old Stig
50 POINTS
And you thought he was dead. Actually he grew gills and started hanging out with a no-good gang of cod. Probably.

Clarkson's Nissan-k
10 POINTS
Warning: may suddenly catch fire when not surrounded by the soft embrace of several gallons of water.

Hammond's VW Damper Van
10 POINTS
Take care with this one, otherwise the flask, tea mugs and Tupperware box of sandwiches will fall out of the kitchenette.

May's Triumph Herald Sailing Boat
10 POINTS
Double points if you can make the main boom swing round and clonk James on the head in an amusing way.

Another moist product from TG TAT Ltd

Top Gear

As *Top Gear* has become more popular, so, inevitably, television stations around the world have got bored of showing repeats of the UK show – especially since all the good stuff goes to Dave and they get left with the ones where Jeremy has more hair and Richard looks about 14. Instead, they want to make their own versions of *Top Gear*. There are strict guidelines about how these sister shows are made, but there is also plenty of leeway to adjust the familiar elements of the British programme to suit a local audience, as this handy table, based on the French version of *Top Gear* with Jeremi Clarkson, Ricard Hammonde et Jacques Mai, will now demonstrate.

Ricard

Jeremi

Jacques

ORIGINAL TOP GEAR SAYS...	**French Top Vitesse says...**
Tonight, a Ferrari, a Lamborghini and a Maserati on our track...	Ce soir, a Peugeot diesel, a Renault diesel and a different kind of Peugeot diesel on our track...
I was the first to arrive.	None of us arrived because we had gone on strike.
Richard was not impressed with James's choice of car.	Ricard set fire to Jacques's choice of car. And then went on strike.
How hard can it be?	The task appeared to be too difficult. So we all went on strike.
The producers then told us to meet up for some challenges.	The producers then reminded us that it was almost August so we all went on holiday.
Oh for God's sake, get a move on Captain Slow.	Wait, you are working far too fast, Captain Slow.
We were ambitious, but rubbish.	We were ambitious, but if anyone questions the outcome we will blow up the studio.
See you next week. Goodnight.	We will not see you next week because there is a general strike and there will be no television for seven days. Au revoir.

JEREMY INTERVIEWS
RICHARD

JC: Right, Hammond, I'm going to interview you.
RH: Go away, I'm busy.

JC: No you're not. You're lounging about on a sofa. How is that in any way 'busy'?
RH: Seriously, sod off.

JC: So that's you being 'busy' is it? Sitting there reading a magazine about off roading?
RH: Yes, this is me being busy.

JC: A magazine that's basically about murderers, for murderers.
RH: Why does being interested in off roading automatically make you a murderer?

JC: It just does. I'm not saying everyone who does off roading is a murderer, but all murderers like off roading.
RH: But they don't.

JC: Charles Manson. I bet he had some Jeep Wrangler with tractor tyres on it.
RH: [sighs] Shall we do this interview then?

JC: Dr Crippen, he loved a Land Rover series 3 short wheelbase with a winch on the front.
RH: Either do this interview or I'm going to leave the room. And when I come back I may have a knife.

JC: A knife? My case rests. Classic murderer behaviour. Or should I say, classic off roader behaviour.
RH: I'm going.

JC: Wait, wait, wait. Here we go. Question 1. Are you, Richard Hammond, a big gaylord? I'm just going to write 'yes'.
RH: For the love of God.

JC: Are you, Richard Hammond, so small that medically you're classed as a dwarf and you can get free shoes from the government?
RH: Right, that's it. I'm going to find something to kill you with.

JC: No, no, no. I'll ask you a proper question.
RH: A proper question? Go on then.

JC: Erm... Why do you, Richard Hammond, like such rubbish cars?
RH: Define rubbish cars.

JC: You know, Morgans and old Land Rovers that smell of dogs...
RH: At least I don't drive around in a ridiculous, show-off Mercedes with stupid, flared wheelarches.

JC: There's nothing ridiculous about my Mercedes.
RH: It's completely ridiculous. And answer me this. Is it not true that the suspension is so stiff that it's basically breaking all of your ancient, creaky bones, but you're too embarrassed to admit that so you just keep driving around in it, even though it's making your life agony? Is that not true?

JC: I ask the questions here.
RH: Well you're not doing a very good job.

JC: I'm doing a literally superb job... of annoying you.
RH: That's true. But I can't be bothered talking to you anymore.

JC: No wait, wait. I'll ask another proper question.
RH: You haven't got any proper questions. I can see your clipboard from here. It's just got a doodle of a horse and MAY IS GAY written on it.

JC: That's because as a trained journalist I don't need to rely on prepared questions.
RH: Come on then, let's do this interview properly.

JC: Right. Do you, Richard Hammond, like off roading, and are you therefore - as an undeniable fact - a murderer?
RH: We're back to this, are we? Fine, and when do I get to interview you? Question 1: Are you a fat, decrepit old man who dresses like a trendy physics tutor with pubic hair loosely stuck to his head?

JC: Actually you don't get to interview me. This works like a chain, so you have to interview James.
RH: Oh God.

EVERYTHING IS POSSIBLE WITH A HAMMER

We all face tricky and delicate challenges in everyday life, and sometimes it can be hard to know the best course of action to take. Unless, of course, you are Jeremy Clarkson, in which case you just unleash sweet claw-headed steel justice upon the problem

HAMMER!

PROBLEM 1:
REPAIRING A FABERGÉ EGG

Ah. Are they still worth a lot of money these days? Oh…

PROBLEM 2:
ASSEMBLING A NUCLEAR BOMB

HAMMER!

Drat. Oh, for God's sake stop making such a fuss! Give it a couple of hundred years and this'll all be good as new. Probably.

PROBLEM 3:
INTERNATIONAL PEACE

HAMMER!

Sorry. Really thought that would work. Still, it was their Prime Minister's fault for leaning forward at the wrong moment.

PROBLEM 4:
SPLITTING THE ATOM

HAMMER!

Bother. Didn't realise all this equipment was that expensive.

PROBLEM 5:
OPEN-HEART SURGERY

HAMMER!

Damn. But he probably would've died anyway.

FORD ESCORT COSWORTH

The Ford Sierra Cosworth bestrode '80s motor-sport like a spoiler-wearing and slightly pikey Colossus, dominating the British Touring Car Championship and World Touring Cars, as well as enjoying some success as a rally car.

Ford decided that 'some success' wasn't enough and set about grafting the mechanical gubbins of the later four-wheel-drive version of the Sierra Cosworth underneath the shell of the new Ford Escort MkV. This wasn't the work of a moment, because the Sierra's engine sat at 90 degrees to the way it would normally fit in an Escort, but they sussed out how to make the whole thing fit

and then Ford bosses commissioned a small design agency in the Midlands to create some suitably lairy looking body-work mods.

Then, since the rules of rallying said you had to sell a minimum number of road-going versions, the Escort Cosworth went on sale at selected Ford dealers. And it was a sensation. In an era before Imprezas and Evos had hit their stride, nothing else offered so much turbo-nutter grunt and four-wheel-drive grip in one pumped-up hatchback body. Some bloke called Jeremy Clarkson used to have an Escort Cossie and he thought it was so amazing he still misses it to this day.

TOP GEAR LISTS

FIVE PLACES JAMES THINKS ARE IN SURREY
Cardiff, Ipswich, Scotland,
the Irish Sea, Greece

**FIVE 'FOREIGN FOODS' THAT RICHARD
VIEWS WITH SUSPICION**
Spaghetti bolognese, fig rolls, Haribo,
flavours of Fanta that aren't orange, bananas

**FIVE NAMES JEREMY WOULD USE IF HE WAS
A SECRET AGENT TRYING TO AVOID DETECTION
WHILST CHECKING INTO A HOTEL**
Jennifer Clarkson, Jeremo Clarksyn,
The Amazing Jezmo, Jesus H. Clarkson, Mrs James May

FIVE TYPES OF MUSIC THE STIG DOESN'T LIKE
Flute fusion, fat bhangra, milky jazz, spoon groove,
the middle bit of 'Rock Me Amadeus' when it goes mental and
appears to turn into a completely different song

**FIVE CARS TOP GEAR CURRENTLY HAS
VERY LITTLE INTEREST IN TESTING**
The HessianTech H12 Peacecrisps, the Greenwash Smugtronic,
the Bellende Malheureusement Electronique,
the Mimsytoss E-2 Cressmatic,
the Lentil Systems GoGreen Hugo Chavez Edition

**FIVE PEOPLE WHO PROBABLY WOULDN'T
RETURN TOP GEAR'S CALLS ABOUT BEING
THE STAR IN THE REASONABLY PRICED CAR**
Jonathan Porritt, Bill Oddie, Ken Livingstone,
Hazel Blears, Michael Jackson

radiotimes.com

31 – 38 September 2009 £0.50

RadioTimes

Some people think *Top Gear* is repeated too much. As these excerpts from a typical day's TV listings show, nothing could be further from the truth.

BBC2

18:00 The Best of Top Gear
Motoring show. A highlights programme themed around cars that have an H in their name.

19:00 Celebrity Extreme Masterchef
This week, Kerry Katona and Nigel Havers attempt to cook a lamb shank, whilst being hosed with machine-gun fire.

20:00 The Best of Top Gear
Motoring show. A highlights programme themed around the word 'raspberries'.

21:00 Ozzy & James's Class A Adventure NEW SERIES
James May and Ozzy Osbourne tour Britain looking for the best in locally-sourced hard drugs. This week, the pair go to Leeds on the hunt for crack.

21:30 The Best of Top Gear
Motoring show. A highlights programme themed around the colour yellow.

Steve

9:00 Top Gear
In this episode, Jeremy shouts, 'Power'.

10:00 Top Gear
In this episode, James does something slowly.

11:00 Top Gear
In this episode, Richard is mocked for being small.

12:00 Top Gear
In this episode, James is the first to arrive.

13:00 Top Gear
In this episode, Jeremy buys an old car and crashes into something.

14:00 Top Gear
In this episode, Richard delivers a piece to camera whilst wearing a waistcoat.

15:00 Top Gear
In this episode, Jeremy does something funny with a hammer.

16:00 Top Gear
In this episode, James wears a stripy jumper.

17:00 Top Gear
In this episode, Jeremy ends a studio link with the words 'How hard can it be?'

18:00 Top Gear
In this episode, Richard is indignant.

19:00 Top Gear
In this episode, James is accused of being pedantic.

20:00 Top Gear
In this episode, Richard has longer hair than he used to have.

21:00 Top Gear
In this episode, Jeremy pauses before saying the last bit of his sentence.

22:00 Top Gear
In this episode, a joke is made about Richard having his teeth whitened.

23:00 Top Gear
In this episode, James appears to get lost.

24:00 Top Gear
In this episode, Jeremy does something with the army.

01:00 Top Gear
In this episode, The Stig is listening to some funny music.

BBC THREE

19:00 Top Gear
Richard has short hair and Jeremy looks less grey so it's probably from an early series, although James is wearing the same stripy jumper so it's hard to tell. There are some cars in it.

20:00 Five Gallons of Cider and a Bucket of Peanuts   NEW SERIES
The inexplicably popular sit-com returns for a 25th series. This week Beano farts audibly whilst Jase and Fabreeze have an argument about their sex life, and the audience literally soils itself laughing at some other things that aren't sodding funny.

20:30 Top Gear
The three presenters buy some old cars and then do some challenges with them. A person who needs to plug a book or film or television show is the Star in the Reasonably Priced Car.

21:30 YOOF!
Hard-hitting young person's drama made by middle-aged people from Chiswick. This week, Damo is concerned that he may have taken some bad drugs whilst Shanice is worried that she may have got chlamydia after having unprotected sex at the same time as downloading music onto her iPod whilst on crack pills during a knife fight.

22:28 Newsfart
All the day's top stories delivered in such a breathlessly hurried way that it's impossible to absorb any of the information being imparted, leaving the viewer with the confused impression that Boris Johnson may have declared war on Janet Jackson in Bhutan.

22:30 Top Gear
A tall man mocks a small man who then mocks another man who is quite slow and has funny hair. Another man drives a small blue car round in circles.

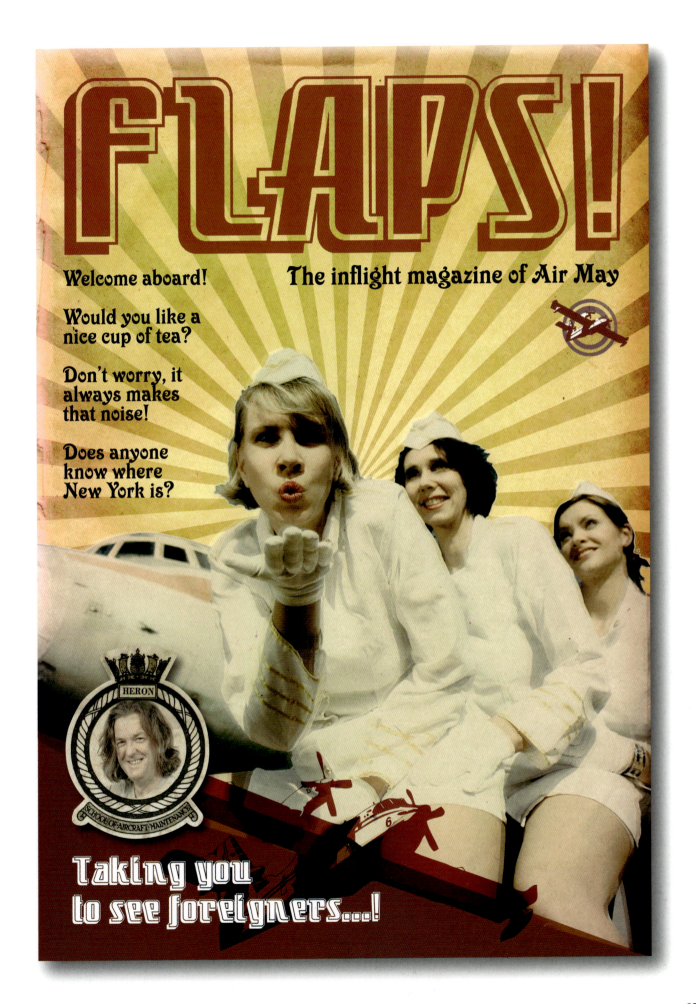

FLAPS!

Welcome aboard!

Would you like a nice cup of tea?

Don't worry, it always makes that noise!

Does anyone know where New York is?

The inflight magazine of Air May

Taking you to see foreigners...!

A word from our founder

Ah, hullo there and welcome aboard. I hope you have a jolly nice time aboard this Air May aeroplane. As you read this your pilot will be going through the pre-flight checks personally laid out by me, so sit back, relax and within a couple of hours he will be almost ready to begin the procedure that will allow him to turn on the engines about an hour or so after that. In the meantime, why not take this opportunity to familiarize yourself with important details about this aircraft, such as where to get a cup of tea, and where to rest that cup of tea once you've got it. If you have any questions, please don't hesitate to pop your head through the cockpit doorway and ask the pilot what's what. I would only ask that you don't do this at times when he needs to concentrate, such as landing, take-off and whilst he is re-filling his pipe. On behalf of everyone at Air May, especially Janet who is writing down this bit as I dictate it, we wish you a safe and pleasantly precise flight. Thank you Janet, I think that ought to do it. Do you think I could have a cup of tea now please? You're ever so kind. Did Archie ever find out why both engines fell off? Really? Oh gosh. Well we'd better hope it was just a one off. Ah, by the way, you can stop taking notes now. I've finished dictating. Thank you.

James May Founder, Air May

In-flight catering

During this flight, a range of drinks and foodstuffs will be served to you by our highly trained hostess ladies or – for smaller aircraft – the pilot. Here is a list of what is on offer:

Food
Steak & kidney pie
Beef Hula Hoops*

Drinks
A cup of tea
A pint of bitter

* Warning: may be substituted for plain Hula Hoops if the shop opposite the airfield has run out of beef ones.

Duty free

During this flight you will be able to buy certain things for at least two shillings less than they would cost you on the ground. Here is a selection of the items on offer:

• **A pipe**
• **Some slacks**
• **A photograph of Douglas Bader**
• **A bottle of bitter**

The fleet

The Bexley-Mountford BM171 'Mountainfinder'

Engines: 2½
Seats: 14 + 20 standing
Range: 48 miles
Did you know? Popular beat musician Buddy Holly never flew on a BM171 because he thought it looked 'too dangerous'!

The Suffolk Aircraft Corporation 733 'Orphanmaker'

Engines: Yes
Seats: Yes
Range: No
Did you know? John Denver wrote his famous song 'Near Death Experience' about this plane!

The Peters Gressingham TA-98D 'Leadballoon'

Engines: 1x Hemsby Massingberg 'Smokemaker' two stroke radial
Seats: 6 x armchairs, 12 x stools
Range: TBC
Did you know? Motor racing legend Graham Hill called the TA-98D 'A one way ticket to pain'!

Our routes

London to Constantinople	London to Peking	London to The French
London to The Americas	London to The Antipodes	London to Surrey

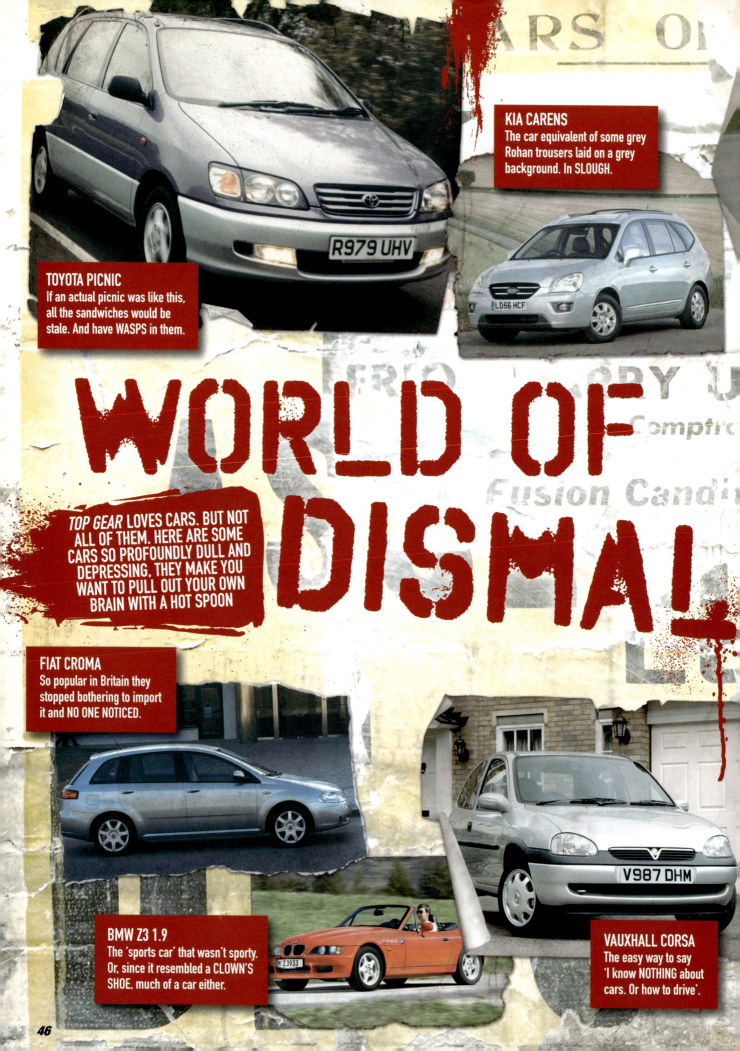

KIA CARENS
The car equivalent of some grey Rohan trousers laid on a grey background. In SLOUGH.

TOYOTA PICNIC
If an actual picnic was like this, all the sandwiches would be stale. And have WASPS in them.

WORLD OF DISMAL

TOP GEAR LOVES CARS. BUT NOT ALL OF THEM. HERE ARE SOME CARS SO PROFOUNDLY DULL AND DEPRESSING, THEY MAKE YOU WANT TO PULL OUT YOUR OWN BRAIN WITH A HOT SPOON

FIAT CROMA
So popular in Britain they stopped bothering to import it and NO ONE NOTICED.

BMW Z3 1.9
The 'sports car' that wasn't sporty. Or, since it resembled a CLOWN'S SHOE, much of a car either.

VAUXHALL CORSA
The easy way to say 'I know NOTHING about cars. Or how to drive'.

FORD ESCORT MKIV
Less a car, more an appliance. And not a very good one. If it was a dishwasher it would cover your plates in VOMIT.

RENAULT 9
The physical embodiment of a DAMP EVENING in downtown Calais.

ALFA ARNA
Japanese styling with Italian reliability. Come on people, that's the WRONG WAY ROUND.

CHRYSLER NEON
Woeful car, with an especially woeful interior. Last time you saw plastic this THIN AND NASTY, it had a CD inside.

HYUNDAI ACCENT
A low-powered, three-cylinder diesel engine? Who thought *that* was a good idea? Presumably someone who DESPISES HUMANITY.

THINGS YOU MAY NOT KNOW ABOUT
THE STIG

• During the 1970s, The Stig enjoyed a brief stint as a nude model.

• The Stig absolutely hates cyclists. 'I absolutely hate cyclists,' he told *The Independent*. 'If they use the roads for free and they don't have to pay any tax, they must obey the rules!' he quips.

• From June until October 1987, The Stig's father was the Lord High Chancellor of Great Britain.

• The Stig drinks two litres of water a day. 'I drink two litres of water a day,' he told *The Times*. 'The drawback is that you have to go to the loo a lot!' he quips.

• In December 2008, The Stig starred as Abanazar in a production of *Aladdin* at the Yvonne Arnaud Theatre in Guildford. *The Surrey Advertiser* described it as 'a sheer delight'.

• The Stig's older brother is called Phil.

• The Stig thinks Castle Drogo in Devon is amazing. 'Castle Drogo in Devon is amazing,' he told *The National Trust Magazine*. 'It's enormous and imposing. It was designed by that great Edwardian architect, Sir Edwin Lutyens, for the self-made millionaire, Julius Drewe!' he quips.

• The Stig's auto-biography was described as 'surprisingly well-written' by *The Scotsman*.

• The Stig's favourite CD to listen to while driving is Martin Jarvis – the actor who played Jeeves in the Broadway show *By Jeeves* – reading P. G. Wodehouse's stories. 'My favourite CD to listen to while driving is Martin Jarvis – the actor who played Jeeves in the Broadway show, *By Jeeves* – reading P.G. Wodehouse's stories,' he told *The Sunday Times*. 'I have them all!' he quips.

• The Stig is rather reluctant to share his favourite holiday destination – Munira Island Camp in Kenya – because it's so special. 'I'm rather reluctant to share my favourite holiday destination – Munira Island Camp in Kenya – because it's so special,' he told the *Daily Telegraph*. 'I could easily spend half the year there!' he quips.

→ Production

Please check this. All these facts appear to be about the actor Nigel Havers. NOT The Stig! Confused?

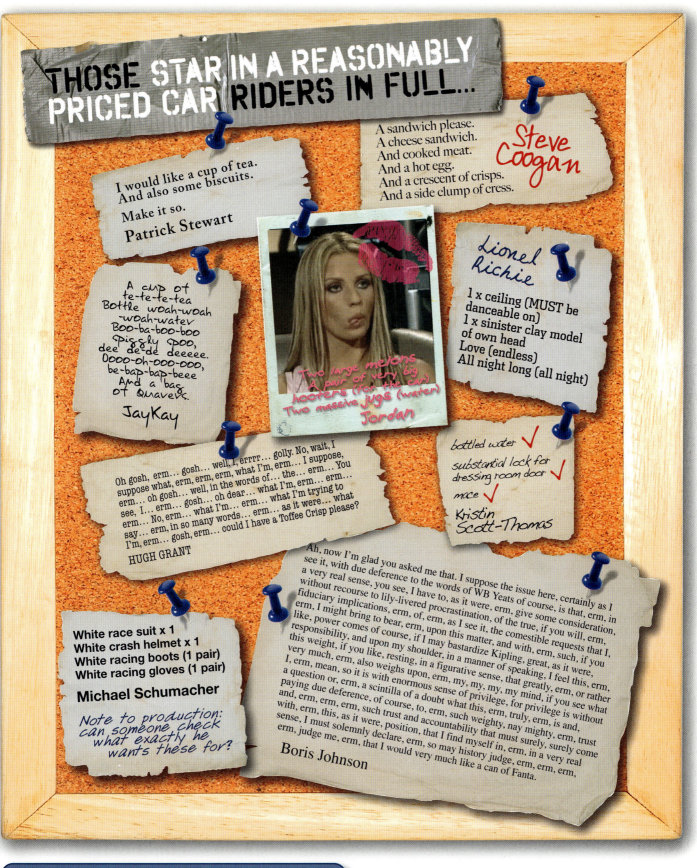

I would like a cup of tea.
And also some biscuits.

Make it so.

Patrick Stewart

A sandwich please.
A cheese sandwich.
And cooked meat.
And a hot egg.
And a crescent of crisps.
And a side clump of cress.

Steve Coogan

A cup of
te-te-te-tea
Bottle woah-woah
-woah-water
Boo-ba-boo-boo
Piggly poo,
dee de-de deeeee.
Oooo-oh-ooo-ooo,
be-bap-bap-beee
And a bag
of Quavers.

JayKay

Two large melons
A pair of very big
hooters (for the car)
Two massive jugs (water)
Jordan

Lionel Richie

1 x ceiling (MUST be
danceable on)
1 x sinister clay model
of own head
Love (endless)
All night long (all night)

Oh gosh, erm... gosh... well, I, errrr... golly. No, wait, I
suppose what, erm, erm, erm, what I'm, erm... I suppose,
erm... oh gosh... well, in the words of... the... erm... You
see, I... erm... gosh... oh dear... what I'm, erm... erm...
erm... No, erm... what I'm... erm... what I'm trying to
say... erm, in so many words... erm... as it were... what
I'm, erm... gosh, erm... could I have a Toffee Crisp please?

HUGH GRANT

bottled water ✓
substantial lock for
dressing room door ✓
mace ✓

*Kristin
Scott-Thomas*

White race suit x 1
White crash helmet x 1
White racing boots (1 pair)
White racing gloves (1 pair)

Michael Schumacher

*Note to production:
can someone check
what exactly he
wants these for?*

Ah, now I'm glad you asked me that. I suppose the issue here, certainly as I
see it, with due deference to the words of WB Yeats of course, is that, erm, in
a very real sense, you see, I have to, as it were, erm, give some consideration,
without recourse to lily-livered procrastination, of the true, if you will, erm,
fiduciary implications, erm, of, erm, as I see it, the comestible requests that I,
erm, I might bring to bear, erm, upon this matter, and with, erm, such, if you
like, power comes of course, if I may bastardize Kipling, great, as it were,
responsibility, and upon my shoulder, in a manner of speaking, I feel this, erm,
this weight, if you like, resting, in a figurative sense, that greatly, erm, or rather
very much, erm, also weighs upon, erm, my, my, my, my mind, if you see what
I, erm, mean, so it is with enormous sense of privilege, for privilege is without
a question or, erm, a scintilla of a doubt what this, erm, truly, erm, is and,
paying due deference, of course, to, erm, such weighty, nay mighty, erm, trust
and, erm, erm, erm, such trust and accountability that must surely, surely come
with, erm, this, as it were, position, that I find myself in, erm, in a very real
sense, I must solemnly declare, erm, so may history judge, erm, erm, erm,
erm, judge me, that I would very much like a can of Fanta.

Boris Johnson

---

myface   Home   Profile   Friends   Inbox

Richard Hammond is now in a
relationship with **Oliver**
20 minutes ago · Comment · Like

myface   Home   Profile   Friends   Inbox

James May updated his date of birth to
16 January, 1923
10 minutes ago · Comment · Like

Making TopGear

THE VIEW FROM A STAR IN THE REASONABLY PRICED CAR
with top movie star
TOM CRUISE

Hey, guys! Tom Cruise here. You probably know me best from movies such as Mission: Impossible, Mission: Impossible II and Mission: Impossible III. But I gotta tell you, making those great motion pictures was nothing to the awesome time I had when I was a guest on the totally awesome Top Gear show.

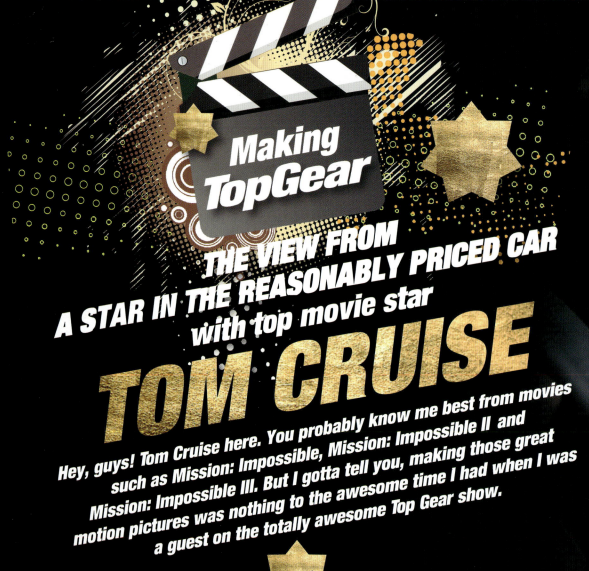

I remember the day that my good friend, TV's James May, called me up and said, 'Hello Tom, it's TV's James May here. Would you like to come onto the *Top Gear* television programme?' Heck, I didn't need to be asked twice! 'TV's James May', I said, 'I'll be there tomorrow!' 'Please don't be there tomorrow,' TV's James May replied. 'It's a Saturday, and there will be no one there. Why don't you come down next Wednesday when we are recording the programme.'

Well, I was so excited I got on the next affordable flight to London, England and checked myself into a Travel Lodge, just next to a little street called the M25. It was awesome. Well I gotta tell you, that Wednesday could not come soon enough. I guess it's fair to say I barely slept at all that Tuesday night and was up real early waiting for the minicab that would take me to

the studio. And as that little Toyota Carina made its way towards Dunsfold, England, I remember thinking, 'You really made it, Tommy boy.'

Heck, I thought *that* was, like, totally amazing, but it was nothing to what happened when my driver finally found the *Top Gear* airfield itself. As soon as I arrived I was shown into the awesome production office and invited to sit down on a couch that was real fancy and I guess was from somewhere awesome like the DFS sale. Then a lady appeared and offered me a tea or coffee. Jeez, I said, what a choice! 'Actually, Jeremy tried to fix the coffee machine earlier and now it's broken. I'll get you a tea...' she replied. Like, totally amazing! Hey, I've been in the movie business for almost 30 years but even I was blown away by what happened next. My tea arrived, and with it came a small plate with two-

'Would I have the fish & chips or the non-specific meat curry? Jeez, it was all too much...'

nd-a-half digestive biscuits on it. Totally freakin' awesome! Even Bruckheimer don't get that!

I was just finishing the tea and wondering where that, like, totally amazing smell of damp was coming from when another lady arrived and told me it was time for my lap in the Reasonably Priced Car. Lemme tell you, this was a moment like no other. It was Academy Award nomination, my wedding and that weird shit I did on Oprah's sofa all rolled into one. At last, I would get to drive a small, Korean-made automobile on the famous *Top Gear* test track! How I had spent so many nights watching Dave on cable and dreaming of this moment. And I gotta tell you, as I walked to that little car, the icy wind blowing across the airfield felt like the warm embrace of a long lost friend, the driving rain soaking my face like a thousand stolen kisses soaking my shirt and pants. As for the car itself – man, all I can say when I got back to the US, I went straight to Beverley Hills Chevrolet and ordered me a Lacetti of my own!

All too soon my laps were over and I returned to the production office where a lady yet again made my

head spin with a choice of awesome food for lunch. Would I have the fish & chips or the non-specific meat curry? Jeez, it was all too much. In the end I had the curry. They'd run out of fish. It was wicked awesome cool. I've worked with Spielberg, Kubrick, Scorsese, but I ain't never had the chance to sit in a draughty and strange-smelling Portakabin somewhere in Surrey, England, eating a tepid curry all to myself! Man, it was totally amazing! Then a lady arrived and told me to 'Hurry up' because it was time to get to the studio. Yes my friends, it was showtime! I guess the rest you know from your television screens, but for me it's the behind-the-scenes moments that will live on in my memory, filed under 'Pure awesomeness'!

CORRECTION: It has been brought to our attention that Tom Cruise has never been a guest on *Top Gear* and the above interview was almost certainly NOT conducted with the star of films such as *Mission: Impossible, Mission: Impossible II* and *Mission: Impossible III*. In fact, we suspect it was just Stig's friend Larsen putting on a silly voice. Sorry.

PEOPLE WHO HAVE COPIED THINGS OFF TOP GEAR

AS *TOP GEAR* HAS BECOME MORE POPULAR, IT'S INEVITABLE THAT PEOPLE WOULD START TO COPY THINGS FROM THE PROGRAMME. SOMETIMES THIS IS FLATTERING. SOMETIMES, HOWEVER, IT'S A BLOODY LIBERTY. HERE WE PRESENT SOME OF THE WORST *TG* THIEVES OF ALL TIME.

CULPRIT 1

Sir Ranulph Fiennes

THE EVIDENCE: *Top Gear* successfully drove to the North Pole in a Toyota pick-up truck. Next thing you know, this so-called 'explorer' has SWIPED this brilliant scheme and is flouncing off to snowy climes, without even having the sense to take a car. Pah!

VERDICT: COPYCAT

CULPRIT 2

The Premier League

THE EVIDENCE: *Top Gear* invents car football, first with Toyota Aygos and then later with VW Foxes. It works well. So well that some unscrupulous people in major towns STEAL the idea and use it to form some sort of 'league', except that they foolishly forget to play their 'football' in cars. Gah!

VERDICT: COPYCAT

CULPRIT 3

The Le Mans 24 Hour

THE EVIDENCE: *Top Gear* has the genius idea of going 24-hour racing. But hang on, what's Johnny Frenchman up to if not shamelessly NABBING this idea and inviting all his mates from Peugeot, Audi and Aston over to have a 24-hour race of his own. Pfffft!

VERDICT: COPYCAT

CULPRIT 4

Sir Michael Parkinson

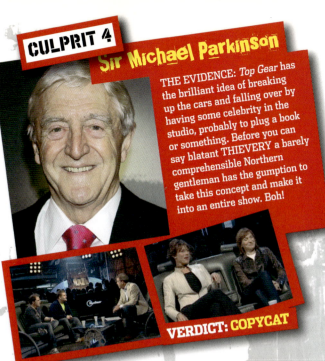

THE EVIDENCE: *Top Gear* has the brilliant idea of breaking up the cars and falling over by having some celebrity in the studio, probably to plug a book or something. Before you can say blatant THIEVERY a barely comprehensible Northern gentleman has the gumption to take this concept and make it into an entire show. Boh!

VERDICT: COPYCAT

CULPRIT 5

The bloke who landed his plane in the Hudson River

THE EVIDENCE: As part of an exhaustive test of British Leyland cars, *Top Gear* fills each one with water. Mere months later, this pilot chap shamelessly NABS such radical thinking and attempts to waterlog his bloody Airbus. There are easier ways to test door sealing Capt. Stealy McStealingman. Pshaw!

VERDICT: COPYCAT

CULPRIT 6

NASA

THE EVIDENCE: *Top Gear* comes up with a radical plan to send a Reliant Robin into orbit. And it almost works. But oh no, that's not good enough for the NASA organization of America. They have to FILCH this advanced thinking and build their own so-called 'Shuttle' then use it to zoom around space acting as if they thought of it all for themselves. Gnnrrr!

VERDICT: COPYCAT

CULPRIT 8

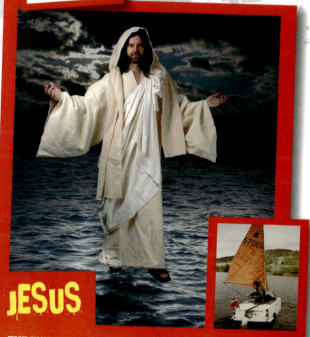

JESUS

THE EVIDENCE: *Top Gear* has a couple of cracks at building amphibious cars and eventually makes a successful crossing of a short bit of sea, something that clearly doesn't escape the attention of a Mr J Christ of Nazareth who PURLOINS the basic concept the next time he fancies getting to the other side of the Red Sea. AND he doesn't even bother using a shabby Nissan pick-up truck. Dah!

VERDICT: We'll let him off this one. Apparently his Dad's quite powerful.

CULPRIT 7

The Great War

THE EVIDENCE: *Top Gear* decides to have a harmless competition with their rivals from the German version of *Top Gear*. And then what happens? The bloody Kaiser POCKETS the whole concept and kicks off with the British, gets the French and Russians and Americans involved, blows the whole lot out of proportion AND doesn't even end it with a race around a track. Then 21 years later they meet for a re-match. Next time, come up with something of your own, Silly Moustache Man. Fnnn!

VERDICT: COPYCAT

Top Gear

Wherever you go in the world, it's pretty certain that you can find an episode of *Top Gear* running on some TV channel or other. But hang on a second, you might think as you sit there watching it. These three buffoons falling over and setting fire to things are somehow different. What you're actually watching is a local version of the *Top Gear* format, made under licence. This happens a lot in TV. For example, the United States makes *Strictly Come Dancing* but calls it *Dancing with the Stars*. And the Venezuelans have replicated *Totally Saturday* by screening footage of a big pile of horse shit. Hence, licensed versions of *Top Gear* are made all around the world, including in the Netherlands where it is presented by Jan Claarkson, Rikki Haammond and Jaap Maay. And, as this handy chart shows, there are a few differences.

Jan

Rikki

Jaap

Around The World

ORIGINAL TOP GEAR SAYS...	Dutch Topp Geear says...
Tonight, we make smoke on our track...	Tonight, we make smoke in a café...
...and we drive a Land Rover up a mountain.	...and we ride a bicycle along an extremely flat, straight road.
How hard can it be? We decided to find out.	How hard can it be? We removed our trousers to show you.
We stopped for petrol.	We stopped for petrol. And some biscuits. And some cheese. And some chocolate. And some crisps. And some more cheese.
I was the first to arrive.	I was the first to arrive. And then I lit a cigarette.
Whilst James fixed his car, Richard and I decided to help by driving off.	Whilst Jaap fixed his car, Rikki and I decided to help by making love.
James ran off the track and onto the grass.	Jaap ran off the track in search of grass.
And on that bombshell, it's time to end.	And on that bongshell, it's, erm... man, I just totally forgot what I was saying.

Ambitious... but really, you know, like totally mellow. Yea maaaan.

El newspaperato numero uno por el community ex-pat hable Español • 21 Mars 2009

EL REPORTERO MALLORCA

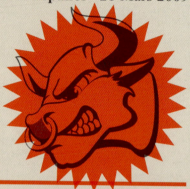

MALLORCA EN TOP GEAR !!

Mucho excitamento esta weekendo as el presentores del Angleterra auto programmo <<*Top Gear*>> arrivada en Mallorca para filmo del Rallye Classico.

El presentores assemblendado en el docko del Palma con tres autos mucho old e crap. Señor Jeremy Clarksonio haveo una MG Midget – <<Es non Midget, esta una Austin-Healey Sprite>> il Clarksonio insistato. Señor Richard Hammondeo haveo una Lanchester fabricado por su grandpadre, e Señor James May haveo una Citroën Ami molto asthmatico.

Mucho amusemento por onlookeratos as el presentores discover ils haveo une co-pilote por el Rallye Classico. Por Señor Clarksonio una experte du rallye no hablo Inglés, por Señor Hammondeo una hombre molto microscopico, e por Señor May una señorita modello glamouroso avec de boobolosos magnifico.

El presentores concernato aboutos el challenge du Rallye Classico mais Señor Clarksonio hablo <<How hardos can es be?>> El answerato es molto hardos! El noteos del pace es uselesso avec una co-pilote silencio e Señor Hammondeo encountero dos problemos: una, ils Lanchester fabricado por su grandpadre run muy picante. E duo, ils co-pilote microscopico non ablo see over el boarda de dash. Meanwhilados, Señor May mucho distractico par de shirt patatas du señorita du Page Tres e el conversationo mucho banal!

Nextos dayos, el presentores avante du el circuito del racing por el finale du Rallye Classico. Una series del lapos timed est una problema por les hombres <<*Top Gear*>>! Señor Clarksonio haveo una clutch knackeratado, Señor Hammondeo haveo els systemos del cooling problemos ongoing, e Señor May molto distractico par de hooteros grande. El tres amigos finito del Rallye Classico nonethelesso e a ca shello du bomb, es is backo del studio!

TORTURA DEL BURRO

Thiso weekos donkey es thrownos off el tower du clock a Caterdral du Santa Maria a 09:00, Saturdaos 28 Mars. Non forgettos!

TORTURA DEL BULL

El bull will getta del stabbing a Las Stadium du Santa Maria a 10:00, Saturdaos 28 Mars. Be thereos ou be una square!

FESTIVAL DEL ANIMALES

El annuale Festival Del Animales es en Saturdaos 28 Mars, commencatos a 11:00 a Del Parc du Santa Maria. As usuales, es est una funos dai outos por el whole famillia avec bull stabbing, donkey throwing, chicken twisting, dog punching e el traditionale machine gunning d'elephant. Bringos del bambinos!

THE COMMIE CARS WE DIDN'T SHOW

When Jeremy and James set out to discover if communists ever made a good car, they assembled an impressive selection of machines from behind what used to be the Iron Curtain. And all of them turned out to be rubbish. But there were some other commie vehicles that they just couldn't get hold of. Here are a few of the Eastern Bloc clunkers they left out...

NVEBGOROD AVTO 3958 C

>> EVERYONE IN NVEBGOROD AVTO'S HOME TOWN OF GZOVGOROV WAS GIVEN 17 MINUTES HOLIDAY AND REWARDED WITH HALF A PORK CHOP

Launched in 1978 after a design process that lasted 56 years, this was Nvebgorod Avto's flagship model, boasting a host of features denied to lesser cars in its range, such as headlights, doors and a fourth wheel.

The 3958's announcement was such an event that it was celebrated with commemorative light bulbs and a personal message of congratulations from the People's Commissariat for Motorized Transportation. Everyone in Nvebgorod Avto's home town of Gzovgorov was given 17 minutes holiday and rewarded with half a pork chop, on the understanding that they would honour the new model by wearing a jovial hat and talking about nothing but the 3958 C for three months.

Sadly, once the three months had elapsed, no actual examples of the 3958 C had been built and it was discovered that the only existing prototype was a crude deception made out of cardboard and powered by six orphans. Its designers were banished to the local zinc mines and the 3958 C was never seen again.

GRAZNOVEZ MECHNICAL WORKS 2833

In 1967, the Soviet central government noticed two separate problems. Firstly, there was a shortage of cars. And secondly, there was a pressing need for more trombones.

The 2833 was the combined solution to both issues. Designed by Graznovez chief engineer Sergei Bagmatov, the 2833 featured the bodywork of a conventional saloon car, which was then surrounded by a complex network of brass pipes that would fulfil the musical part of its design criteria. Innovation abounded, not least in the clever 'slider' mechanism that acted as both the gear lever and the device with which one could change the pitch of the instrument.

Despite its ingenious design, however, the 2833 was not without some substantial problems. First of all, State authorities ruled that it could not be driven at night due to the dreadful and anti-social noise it made at speeds over 4kph. And secondly, anyone who owned one would soon rue its dual nature when they realized they could not use it to get anywhere on days when their children had a school music lesson.

By 1973, the Graznovez had become deeply unpopular as even car-starved Soviets objected to driving something that made a noise like an atonal donkey fart. There were also concerns that the 2833's dual role, allied to its confusing control layout, had resulted in almost 400 Russian children being run over during orchestra rehearsals. By 1975, production had ceased after only 5.9 million had been made.

ZHIVBRIVENZHENETIV 609

The Zhivbrovenzhenetiv People's Motor Factory was set up in 1957 to bring employment to an area that had suffered when the local gymnastics training facility was razed to the ground on the order of Soviet central government following the discovery of an Eddie Cochran record in some nearby woods. The 47,500 employees of the new Zhivbrovenzhenetiv company had no experience of making cars, but what they lacked in knowledge they more than made up for with enthusiasm, as every single one of them pitched in to help with their first model.

Sadly, this proved to be the 609's undoing as it rapidly emerged that this was a small car packed with 47,500 different ideas. The Zhivbrovenzhenetiv was instantly recognizable thanks to its distinctive rectangular tail light and the shape of its saloon car body, which was also an estate. State officials were horrified at such creative thinking from the workers, immediately digging a massive hole outside the factory and forcing every single employee to sit at the bottom of it welding prosthetic limbs whilst they reflected on their foolish and decadent mistake.

With no one left to make the cars, the 609's life was at an end after a mere four months and the production of just 1.3 million vehicles.

3021 AVTO DNIPROPETROVSKIV

Even under Soviet control, the Ukraine always had a fiercely independent streak and nowhere was this more obvious than in Ukrainian-made vehicles like the legendary Avto Dnipropetrovskiv 3021 'Ocnrk'.

Whilst most Eastern Bloc cars of the late '70s chased modernity and reached for the brave new technological world of the '80s, the 3021 was a deliberately retro effort, mimicking the appearance, the handling characteristics and the smell of a donkey. In this respect it was a huge success, especially its long and lumpen bonnet and its famous inability to achieve speeds above 5kph.

The engineers at Avto Dnipropetrovskiv always denied that it was their intention to make a car so donkey-like that many owners found its two-cylinder, 706cc engine would actually run quite happily on carrots, but there was no doubt that when it came to handling, this was a car with an asinine mind of its own. In fact, this was the 3021's downfall, as the state authorities became concerned about the number of casualties caused by the car's sometimes erratic cornering abilities. So, in 1980 they ordered production to cease, just two days after the Ocnrk had killed its 57,000th driver.

WORKER'S KETTLE FACTORY (FAZ) 4011

In 1973, the Soviet Central Planning Committee noticed that everyone in the USSR already had a kettle, except for those who had been found guilty of thinking about the rock band Slade and who had their kettles smashed by the secret police as punishment. As a result of this 'saturacija chajnika' – 'kettle saturation' – the Worker's Kettle Factory in Monchegorsk, near Murmansk in northern Russia, was ordered to turn its hand to car production. Using all of their know-how, the engineers worked at breakneck speed, and by 1984 the first production cars were ready, boasting a distinctive copper body shell and unusual 'viewing trumpet' on the front instead of a windscreen.

While Soviets were loathe to complain about any opportunity to own a car, there was some consternation amongst those who took delivery of a FAZ 4011 and found it not only hard to see out of, but also rather hard to enter in the first place, on account of its one circular door mounted on top of the body, just under the quirky 'centre arch', which curved above the car itself. Some 4011 drivers also complained that the interior was prone to getting 'extremely hot and quite steamy'. Nonetheless, the 4011 was very well regarded in the last days of the USSR, to the extent that Russian journalist Alexey Kazmirov was banished to a local nickel mine for daring to suggest that it was 'just a massive kettle'.

609 452
ZHIVЬRIVENZHENETIV

The fact that Poland was under Soviet control was not going to stop the plucky Polish car industry from announcing its first new car in 47 years and, sure enough, in 1970 that's just what they did as Polski Lejland took the covers off the mighty Znzgna (pronounced 'Cheesecake'). The Znzgna was a revolution in Polish car design, promising advanced design features such as 'window made of glass', 'up to three cylinder in engine', and 'seat for driver'. Sadly, by showcasing such radical new technology, Polski Lejland had clearly made life hard for themselves and the Znzgna was slow to reach eager Polish drivers.

Among the problems discovered during pre-production testing were a tendency for the door to come open, and severe instability caused by the radical fitment of brakes to just the left-hand-side wheels. It was also noted that, while the standard fitment of a driver's seat was a thoughtful touch, it probably should have been fixed to the floor in some way. Determined to remedy all such problems, or in the case of the massive unexplained engine fires, at the very least hush them up, Polski Lejland delayed production until it could bodge its way out of trouble. The net result of this is that the Znzgna did not go on sale until 1998, by which time Poland was a free market and nobody wanted a car that looked like it had been made from old kitchen units.

»

THE ZNZGNA WAS A REVOLUTION IN POLISH CAR DESIGN, PROMISING ADVANCED DESIGN FEATURES SUCH AS 'WINDOW MADE OF GLASS', 'UP TO THREE CYLINDER IN ENGINE', AND 'SEAT FOR DRIVER'

WHO IS THE STIG?

6'6"

6'0"

5'6"

5'0"

4'6"

3'6"

3'0"

alain prost

COULD BE THE STIG BECAUSE...
PROBABLY SMELLS A BIT
GARLICKY, JUST LIKE STIG.

BUT PROBABLY ISN'T BECAUSE...
STIG SEEMS TO GET A RASH
WHENEVER HE GOES TO FRANCE.

david coulthard

COULD BE THE STIG BECAUSE...
PROBABLY LIKES BAGPIPE MUSIC,
BEING SCOTTISH AND ALL THAT.

BUT PROBABLY ISN'T BECAUSE...
STIG ACTUALLY SEEMS TO LIKE
EDDIE JORDAN.

nigel mansell

COULD BE THE STIG BECAUSE...
EMITS A DULL DRONING SOUND,
NOT DISSIMILAR TO THE ONE
THAT COMES OUT OF STIG'S
HELMET SOMETIMES.

BUT PROBABLY ISN'T BECAUSE...
STIG'S VIEWS ON MOUSTACHES
ARE TERRIFYINGLY ANGRY.

james may

COULD BE THE STIG BECAUSE...
ENJOYS MANY OF SAME FOODS
AS STIG, CHIEFLY BEEF HULA
HOOPS AND WINE GUMS.

BUT PROBABLY ISN'T BECAUSE...
STIG DRIVES FAST.

A look at some likely suspects

jodie kidd

COULD BE THE STIG BECAUSE... LIKES JEREMY, KNOWS HOW TO GET TO THE *TOP GEAR* TRACK.

BUT PROBABLY ISN'T BECAUSE... STIG ISN'T THAT TALL. DOESN'T SMELL THAT NICE EITHER.

michael schumacher

COULD BE THE STIG BECAUSE... DON'T BE RIDICULOUS.

jackie stewart

COULD BE THE STIG BECAUSE... APPEARED ON *TOP GEAR*, SEEMED TO KNOW QUITE A LOT ABOUT JAMES ALREADY.

BUT PROBABLY ISN'T BECAUSE... STIG HAS NEVER BEEN SEEN DRESSED ALL IN TARTAN LIKE A NOVELTY DOLL FROM AN EDINBURGH TOURIST SHOP.

robbie williams

COULD BE THE STIG BECAUSE... HAS MYSTERIOUSLY DISAPPEARED FROM PUBLIC VIEW.

BUT PROBABLY ISN'T BECAUSE... STIG'S LAST ALBUM ACTUALLY SOLD QUITE WELL.

6'6"
6'0"
5'6"
'0"
'6"
4'0"
3'6"
3'0"

CARS WE LOVE

JAGUAR XJR

Modern Jags are all very nice, and at their best still have that sense that to drive one you have to be a bit roguish, a bit caddish, a bit Terry Thomas or the *The Fast Show*'s 13th Duke of Wybourne. But nothing quite matches the original gentleman thug in their back catalogue, the old supercharged XJR.

Like many of the most thinly moustached and morally dubious Jaguar drivers, the old XJ was getting on a bit. But that didn't stop its creators dropping in a supercharged straight-six engine that made it go like a leathery rocket and sound like an angry Spitfire.

Then they introduced an even meatier V8, still with the supercharger, that saw the old beast into its dotage. Yes, it was dated but it was also fast and charismatic and – crucially – somehow a little bit naughty. Put it this way, Hannibal Lecter had one. And he was a charming chap that you could never entirely trust. In other words, a perfect Jaaaag man.

RICHARD INTERVIEWS
JAMES

RH: Hello James.
JM: Hello Richard Hammond.

RH: So, I'm supposed to interview you now.
JM: Yes, so I gather.

RH: In which case, would you mind not doing the crossword?
JM: Well, you're not ready yet. You haven't got a note pad. Or a pen. I've got some pens here if you need one.

RH: I don't need a pen; it's on tape.
JM: Hmm. I wouldn't do that. You can't entirely trust electrical things.

RH: No, YOU can't entirely trust electrical things because you're strange.
JM: There's nothing strange about it.

RH: I'm sorry, you're the man who says he 'doesn't believe in electricity'. That's just strange.
JM: But I don't believe in electricity. No one can explain how it works; therefore it's not to be trusted.

RH: But people CAN explain how it works.
JM: Who?

RH: I don't know; electricians, probably. I'm not getting into this again. Shall we start the interview?
JM: Are you going to be asking questions of a philosophical nature?

RH: Yes James, I'm going to be setting you some really philosophical questions.
JM: Really?

RH: No, you twat. That was sarcasm.
JM: So the questions will be of a personal nature? I was afraid of that. I don't really like revealing too much about myself.

RH: You 'don't like revealing too much about yourself'? Yesterday you took the time to tell me precisely when and where you were going to have a dump.
JM: That's different.

RH: No, it isn't. What did you expect me to do with that information? 'Is that the *Daily Telegraph*? I wish to inform you that James May will be evacuating his bowels in five minutes in the loos by the car park near the studio.'
JM: You're just being fatuous now.

RH: OK, I'm going to ask you a question.
JM: Good.

RH: Hang on... Oh no. James. Please stop touching my leg...
JM: Eh?

RH: Stop it. Stop trying to feel me up again.
JM: What are you talking about?

RH: Get your hands off me.
JM: My hands aren't anywh... oh, I get it. So when they transcribe the tape, it'll sound like I'm molesting you. Funny.

RH: I thought so.
JM: Well, you're wrong.

RH: What are you doing?
JM: Waiting for you to stop cocking around and get on with this interview.

RH: No, you're arranging those pens in order of size and colour.
JM: Yes, and what's wrong with that?

RH: What's wrong with it? I don't know where to begin.
JM: By being quiet?

RH: Hilarious. No really, my sides have just split open.
JM: If you're not going to interview me properly, I've got to go. Apparently I have to interview The Stig.

RH: Go on then. See you later.
JM: But first, a spot of Quality Gentleman's Lavatory Time...

TG SUPERCUTS

As you sit there watching Dave, it can be hard to know which series of *Top Gear* the endlessly repeated show you're watching is from. But with this handy hairstyle chart you need wonder no more.

Series

1 2 3 4 5 6 7 8 9 10 11 12 13 14

JEREMY (Lionel Richie ↕ Frizzy pubes)

Full-bodied, if a bit pube-like. Like Lionel Richie, if he was a bit crap and lived near Oxford.

Thinning. But still pube-like. As if Lionel Richie had been rubbing his head too much.

Getting a bit thinner, with some patches of grey. Not dissimilar to the effect that would be achieved if Lionel Richie had been painting his house carelessly without a hat on.

Larger patches of grey appearing. As if a slowly balding Lionel Richie had made a half-arsed effort to attend a fancy-dress party as a badger.

1 2 3 4 5 6 7 8 9 10 11 12 13 14

RICHARD (Duran Duran ↕ Take That)

Short, neat, immaculately gelled. Like the one all the girls fancy from a B-list boy band.

As left, with just a hint of expanding sideburnery. Like the one all the girls fancy from a boy band when they're doing their 'more rocky' third album.

Getting increasingly untamed. Like the one all the girls fancy from a boy band when he's pretending to be a 19th century hero for their overblown new video.

Oh Good Lord! Completely out of control now! Like the one all the girls used to fancy from a boy band that has now quit the band, bought a farm and an acoustic guitar and gone slightly weird.

1 2 3 4 5 6 7 8 9 10 11 12 13 14

JAMES (Cocker Spaniel ↕ King Charles Spaniel)

Spaniel.

Spaniel.

Spaniel.

Spaniel.

30 second guide to...

MERCEDES

Top Gear's quick* guide to one of the world's greatest car makers

So one day a bloke called Mr Benz was a bit bored, so he decided to invent the car, and this went down pretty well, especially with his local taxi company, who liked what they saw and asked him for more, preferably with a lemon fragrance air freshener, which was a problem because at this point there was nowhere to put it, until Mr Benz's mate Mr Daimler (no relation) came along and helped him invent the rear view mirror, and after that they decided to go into business to supply cars to the taxi companies of the world, until they came up with a bigger model and got a call from an evil dictator in Africa who said he wanted one, and once that happened basically every mad despot in the world wanted one, and Mr Benz and Mr Daimler (who by now had become a woman and changed his name to Mercedes) became very rich and were able to die whilst their company carried on.

*And factually incorrect

Instructions for the May-Nav
Satellite Navigation System

Oh, hullo. Thank you for buying this May-Nav Satellite Navigation System. If it wouldn't be too much of an inconvenience, let's run through some basic steps to get you started with this state-of-the-art device. Please remember to make yourself a nice cup of tea before reading any further.

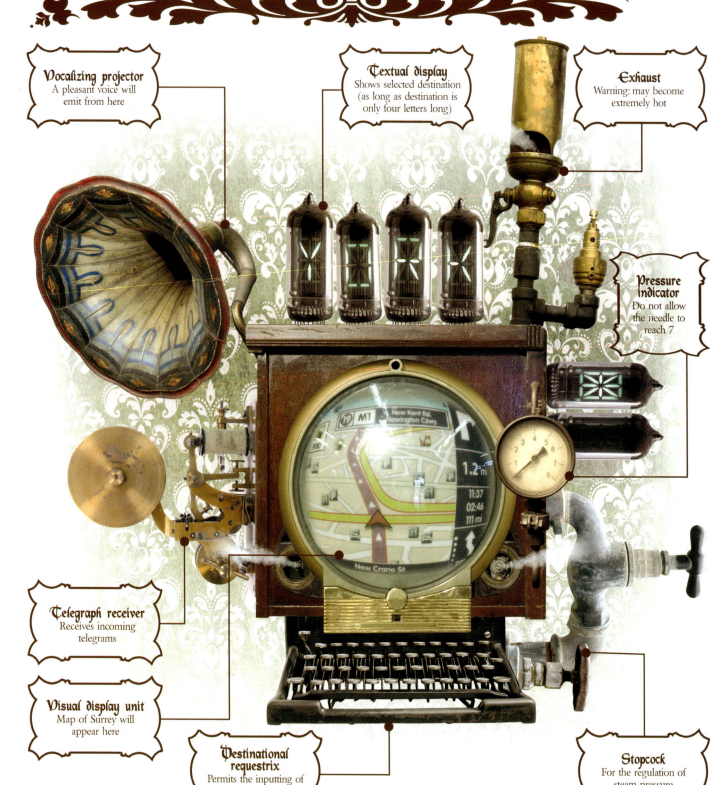

Vocalizing projector
A pleasant voice will emit from here

Textual display
Shows selected destination (as long as destination is only four letters long)

Exhaust
Warning: may become extremely hot

Pressure indicator
Do not allow the needle to reach 7

Telegraph receiver
Receives incoming telegrams

Visual display unit
Map of Surrey will appear here

Destinational requestrix
Permits the inputting of directional requests

Stopcock
For the regulation of steam pressure

To begin, you need to switch on the May-Nav. Do this by turning that hand crank on the lower right of the device until you feel the motor catch.

Once the device has started up, the screen will show you the welcome prompt: 'How are you?' Press either 'Yes, I'm very well, thank you' or 'A bit under the weather actually, but mustn't grumble. How are you?' The device will display the message: 'Not bad, thank you'.

Remember to drink your tea before it gets cold

1 The device will now ask you to select where in Surrey you would like to go. For this example, we are going to ask if it would mind awfully taking us to York.

2 We have now typed in York and the device is asking us: 'Is that near Exeter?' Select either 'I think so' or 'I'm not really sure'. The device will then display the message: 'Sorry, I've completely forgotten where you wanted to go. Did you say Reykjavík?'

3 Re-enter 'York'. The device will then display the message: 'Calculating the route to York, in Surrey'.

If you have finished your tea, go and get another cup from the pot

4 Tidy up the study. Go for a short walk. Listen to the wireless for a bit.

5 The device has now calculated your route and will display the question: 'Would it be acceptable if we started now?' Select 'Yes please, that would be lovely' if you would like guidance to start now. Select 'Would you mind awfully hanging on for a moment' if you are still finishing your tea.

6 If you have selected 'Yes please, that would be lovely', guidance will now start. The screen will display the message: 'Continue straight for about five or six miles or so'

7 Continue to follow the on-screen instructions. The device will display the message: 'Oh dear, you seem to have forgotten your driving gloves'. Turn around and return home to fetch your driving gloves.

8 Once you have retrieved your driving gloves, continue to follow the on-screen instructions. The device will offer simple route guidance, such as 'Turn left', 'Turn right', 'Oh dear, this doesn't look familiar at all' and 'Ah, cock. I was hoping this would turn out to be the M4'.

9 After 15 minutes the device will show the message: 'I think it might be time for a cup of tea'. Select either 'By crikey, you're right' or 'Quite so, I'm parched'.

Stop for a cup of tea

10 When you have completed your tea stop, continue to follow the on-screen instructions. These will include 'Take the third exit at the roundabout', 'Make a U-turn where possible', 'Now I'm almost certain we'll be able to see the sea at any moment... oh blast, I must have been thinking of somewhere else'.

11 The device will display the message: 'I'm terribly sorry about this'.

12 The device will display the message: 'Remember to eat the packet of beef Hula Hoops you have in your bag'.

13 When you have finished your Hula Hoops, continue to follow the on-screen instructions. These will include: 'Make another U-turn in the place where you turned around earlier on', 'Blimey, look at that lovely old Singer Gazelle' and 'I really can't apologize enough for this. Shall we just head back the way we came and ask that old man if he knows where it is?'.

14 You have now arrived at Aberdeen, in Surrey.

Please remember to turn off the device to allow the valves to cool down

FERRARI

Top Gear's quick* guide to one of the world's greatest car makers

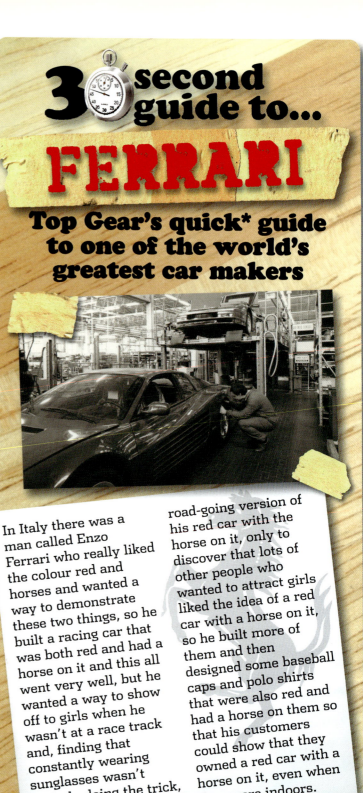

In Italy there was a man called Enzo Ferrari who really liked the colour red and horses and wanted a way to demonstrate these two things, so he built a racing car that was both red and had a horse on it and this all went very well, but he wanted a way to show off to girls when he wasn't at a race track and, finding that constantly wearing sunglasses wasn't entirely doing the trick, he decided to make a road-going version of his red car with the horse on it, only to discover that lots of other people who wanted to attract girls liked the idea of a red car with a horse on it, so he built more of them and then designed some baseball caps and polo shirts that were also red and had a horse on them so that his customers could show that they owned a red car with a horse on it, even when they were indoors.

*And potentially rather misleading

Looking for breakdown cover? Not in a hurry? Eager to hear a lengthy technical explanation of just what the problem is?

JOIN THE MAY-A

All May-A members receive the following benefits:

- **Someone to have a jolly good go at fixing your car**
- **Pleasant chats about the weather**
- **25 per cent off all pies at the nearest petrol station**
- **A free pipe and a pouch of good-quality tobacco**
- **Plenty of time to watch all the cars that haven't broken down going past as you wait for your patrolman to reach you**

Whenever you've got a problem with your car, simply call Hammersmith 212 and a friendly chap in a brown coat will get ready to leave the house and then, once he's made sure all his tools are in the right order, he will head in the wrong direction for a bit before eventually wending his way to your location, perhaps stopping for a lovely pub lunch along the way. And you can be assured that when he finally reaches you he won't simply rush headlong into trying to fix the problem, but will give you a lengthy and extremely not-interesting explanation of what he thinks the problem is in such enormous and complex technical detail that you will probably struggle not to slip gently into a coma.

To our members we're the seventh emergency service.

Just after the St John Ambulance and those people who help you look for lost tortoises.

CALL: 07700 900 212

If it's cheesy and round, it's at your door!

Bongo **PIZZA** Deliveries

020434072

23 October 2001

Dear The Stig,

It is with regret that I have to terminate your empl[oyment]
no longer required as a pizza delivery rider.

While I have been very impressed with the speed
extracting performance from the delivery scoo[ter]
I am highly disappointed that you ignored warni[ngs]
We have endured repeated complaints from cust[omers]
food arriving late and cold. At the heart of this [matter]
by repeatedly lapping the ring road, you [were]
shaving two-tenths off your time. I am th[erefore]
and please return all the meats you have [...]

Yours sincerely,

Alan Flapcock

Alan Flapcock
Regional manager, Bongo Pizza

Taking away the bins
and having long meetings
in **YOUR** community

NORT[H]

6 November 2001

Dear The Stig,

You are hereby dismissed as a lawnmower tractor driver with i[...]

Whilst North Leafbrooke Council will always try to have a full and fra[nk]
feel our discussions with you have always been rather one-sided an[d]
uncommunicative attitude.

I would remind you that cutting grass is not simply about how fast th[e]
certain standards that should be adhered to, specifically that cutting [grass]
and mown in lines not, as you appeared to assume, round and roun[d]
and the entire cricket pitch was ruined as a result. This sort of behav[iour]
which if anything made it worse, and was certainly very upsetting fo[r]

I wish you the best of luck for the future.

Yours sincerely,

Roger Bumhat

Roger Bumhat
General Manager (Maintenance Division)

FRAMLINGCHESTER AMBULANCE SERVICE

Getting you to hospital before it falls off

21 November 2001

Dear The Stig,

With regret I am writing to inform you that as of this [...]
no longer require your services as an ambulance driver [...]

Whilst I have no doubt that speed is a great quality t[...]
driver, this speed has to be coupled with prompt arriva[...]
not repeatedly circling the roundabout outside the hosp[...]
shave another few tenths of a second off your time and [...]
ability to ignore the terrified screams from the back. [...]

Thank you for all your work for Framlingchester Ambulan[...]

Yours sincerely,

Mike Cheese
Operations Manager,
Framlingchester Ambu[...]

BLACK & SOLEMN

Funeral Directors
23 Stiffold Street, **Easby-by-Water, Surrey**

7 December 2001

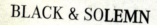

Dear The Stig,
It is with some sadness that I must relieve you of your duties as hearse driver with this company, with immediate effect.

As I have attempted to explain to you several times, when taking part in a funeral cortège, the hearse must maintain a slow and dignified pace. It is wholly unacceptable for the coffin-bearing vehicle to attempt to race other cars and, as you are no doubt well aware, many mourners find it deeply troubling to discover that the deceased is late arriving at the church or crematorium because they are still furiously circling the bypass as the hearse driver attempts to beat his previous 'lap time'.

Also, despite repeated warnings, you signa[...]
white suit is totally inappropriate fo[...]
and Biblical quantities of vomit whic[...]

Yours sincerely,

DONALD BLACK

Donald Black

EAFBROOKE COUNCIL

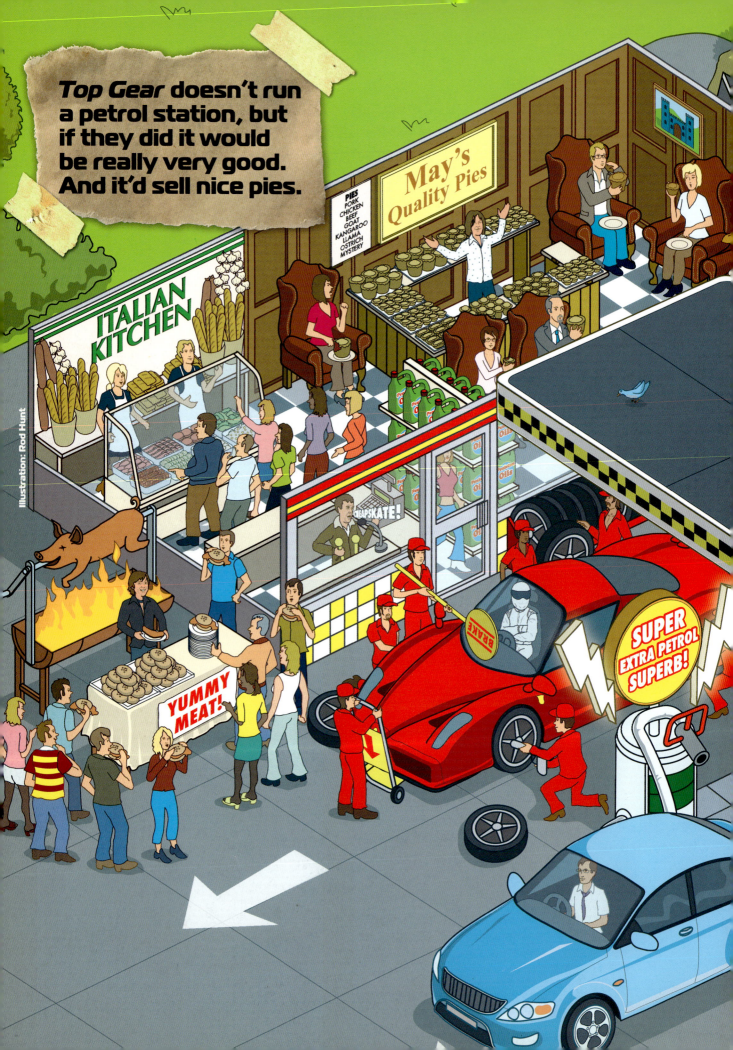

THE STIG

JM: Right, so Stig, I'm going to interview you now.
STIG:

JM: Hm, yes. I have a feeling this might be rather tricky. You're not the most loquacious bloke I've ever met.
STIG:

JM: Um, well perhaps you could write down your answers?
STIG:

JM: Would that work? Um, no. Perhaps not. Erm...
STIG: I like your hair, James.

JM: What?
STIG: I like your hair, James.

JM: Good Lord, you're speaking...
STIG: Do you use a conditioner or just shampoo?

JM: This is extraordinary. What on earth prompted you to break your silence after all this time?
STIG: It's you James. I like your T-shirt. The Hawker Hurricane is one of my favourite aeroplanes too. I would like to see you wearing a thong James. Why not put on a thong and sort of mince around... [muffled giggles]

JM: HAMMOND!
STIG: No James, it's me. Stig. I love you and... [more giggles]

JM: I can see your head moving behind the sofa. Get out from down there.
RH: Hello James.

JM: And what's this? A Hoover pipe?
RH: To, erm, do the spooky Stig voice.

JM: Yes, yes, very good. I suppose you think that's terribly clever don't you?
RH: No... well, yes actually. You have to admit, it was quite funny.

JM: Well it wasn't. You're lucky The Stig seems to be completely unfazed by your cockendery. Look at him, just sitting there.
STIG: I just want to be your friend, James.

JM: Clarkson, I know you're behind there too, you know.
STIG: I don't know what you mean James. Touch my helmet James...
RH: You might as well come out, he's onto us.
JC: Really? Oh.

JM: You two are the biggest pair of clots I've ever met. I mean really, have you not got anything better to do?
JC: Better than annoying you? Nnnnnno.

JM: And you've ruined my interview.
RH: Your interview with The Stig? He was hardly going to be the most chatty subject, was he?
JC: That well-known anecdotalist, The Stig.

JM: You never know, I might have got him to talk.
JC: And you did James, you did.

JM: No, I got two complete cocks with the tube off an old vacuum cleaner to talk. And frankly, I hear enough of you two rabbiting on as it is.
JC: Would you like us to leave?

JM: Yes. Go on, get out.
RH: Remember, Stig loves you James.
JC: Especially in a thong. Or maybe it's the other way around...

JM: Get out!
RH: Bye bye.

JM: I do apologize Stig. Sadly my colleagues are a pair of total arses.
STIG: Mincemeat.

JM: Erm... chaps...

Look at our latest range of handy applications.
LOOK AT THEM.

Pocket Poweeeeer™
For when you can't be bothered to shout POWEEEEER this useful download will do it for you. Features three volume settings: loud / Concorde on take off / ouch, something in my ear has burst.

You're Right!™
Simply ask it a difficult question then give it the answer you know in your mind to be correct and it will reply with 'You're right, Jeremy'.

iHammer™
Turns your phone into a hammer. *Warning:* your phone will almost certainly get bits of nail and wood in it and become broken.

Portable Bombshell™
The very latest development from Clarksoft. Activate **Portable Bombshell™** simply by shaking your phone and it will instantly come up with a contrived piece of barely shocking news that will allow you to leave any meeting, drinks party or dinner engagement on a high note.

Co-presenter Mockmatic™
There are times when you're too busy to tell Richard that he's microscopic or remind James that he's too pedantic. Now, this invaluable application will do it for you. Simply set the timer and, at pre-set intervals, your phone will ring them and shout MIDGET! or SPANIEL-HAIRED DULLARD! at them.

Clarksoft™
LITERALLY the best phone software... in the world

TANK TOP GEAR

PILOT EPISODE script version 2

TITLES MENU	TITLES **JEREMY** voice over: Tonight, Richard drives the new Scirocco R20… in a tank top. Can you powerslide the new Gallardo… in a tank top? And Donald Sinden is the star in a reasonably priced tank top.
STUDIO LINK 1	**JEREMY** (wearing a tank top): Hello, and welcome. Now, every year in Britain over 50,000 people have an attack of faecal urgency whilst driving. And that gave the producers an idea. What's the best car for someone who suffers rectal leakage and is on a tight budget? **RICHARD** (wearing a tank top): Yep, so they gave us each £1,000 the[…] to go out and find a car with vinyl sea[…] some other easily wipe-able material.[…] **JAMES** (wearing a tank top) We were told to scoff a massive bowl[…] and prunes then meet up at the track[…] who had got the best deal…
VT 1	VT
STUDIO LINK 2	**JEREMY** (wearing a tank top): That didn't go entirely as planned. **RICHARD** (wearing a tank top): It didn't, did it? **JAMES** (wearing a tank top): I still can't sit down properly. **JEREMY** (wearing a tank top): Anyway, we'll pick that up later on. But now it's time to do the news… …while wearing tank tops.

WHAT'S ON TV?

SNEAK OFF FOR A POO MAGAZINE   22 APRIL 2008

and then smashes Bill Oddie in the face with a dead crow! Also on BBC2 on Sunday evening is a new spin-off from the ever-popular *Top Gear* series. Entitled *Top Ghee* (BBC2, 8pm), the new show promises to take a typically irreverent look at cars and Indian clarified butter. This week, Jeremy Clarkson tries to drive a lap of the track whilst his hands are covered in ghee, Richard Hammond looks for the best hot hatchback for someone who needs to transport lots of ghee, and James May does his best to avoid being sick as he is driven around the famous Silverstone racetrack by Japanese F1 legend, Taki Inoue, after forcing down an entire tub of ghee. Plus Angela Lansbury is the Star in a Reasonably Priced Vat of Ghee.

THE GUILDFORD EVENING BADGER

THE *TOP GEAR* CIRCUS COMES TO TOWN!

We're used to the crazy exploits of *Top Gear*, otherwise known as presenters Jeremy Clackson, Richard Hamode and James Hay, but this week Guildford plays host to the recording of a unique spin-off show that promises to meld the usual wackiness of the BBC2 motoring show with the good old-fashioned charm of the circus!

Dubbed *Big Top Gear*, the show is to be filmed on Wednesday this week in the enormous circus tent that many Guildfordians will have noticed being erected on the Nigel Havers Playing Fields behind St Cuthbert's church.

At the moment the exact contents of *Big Top Gear* are a closely guarded secret, but a BBC spokesman did hint that there will be something for everyone who likes things to do with cars, clowns, animals and a seal that can balance things on its nose.

The BBC was unable to confirm as yet how many episodes of *Big Top Gear* will be recorded or when the programme will be transmitted.

GODALMING 'WOLF ATTACKS' TRACED TO HAIRY MAN

The wolf that has been terrorizing residents of Godalming and parts of Busbridge with repeated reports of growling in bushes and slight biting has been revealed to, in fact, be a very hairy man.

BBC PREVIEW SCREENING

JEREMY CLARKSON
RICHARD HAMMOND, JAMES MAY
star in the new spin-off show from the makers of *TOP GEAR*

TOP BEAR

In the first show, Jeremy tests a brown bear on the track, Richard compares a grizzly bear to a black bear, and the boys find out if James really is slower than a koala bear. Plus, Bear Grylls is the Star On A Reasonably Priced Bear.

BBC   TV Show Recording

284673000

TOP GRRRRRRRR
The new show devoted to cars and being angry with Richard Hammond

Admit one
**Wednesday 6 May 2009
Dunsfold Aerodrome,
Surrey, England**

Terms & conditions apply: See reverse for details

BBC   Admit one
Wednesday 6 May 2009
Dunsfold Aerodrome, Surrey, England

30 second guide to...

PORSCHE

Top Gear's quick* guide to one of the world's greatest car makers

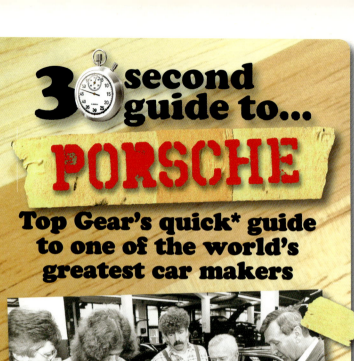

Ferdinand Porsche was a German man who liked things backwards, which is why, when a Mr Hitler asked him to design a car, he put the engine at the back, which Mr Hitler didn't seem to mind although this was because Mr Hitler later turned out to be mad and evil and was driven from power by the British whilst Ferdinand went away to work on his backwards car idea, and decided it would be even more exciting if it was a sports car, although one that would still be based on his original designs for Mr Hitler, who was thankfully now dead so he couldn't complain about anything, unlike customers for Ferdinand's new backwards sports car who sometimes did complain, mostly about how the backwards sports car wasn't very good on a wet road and sometimes made them drive through a hedge, backwards.

*And frankly a bit dubious

...THAT DIDN'T MAKE IT

Tank-Top Gear pilot

From: j.pointishoes@bbc.com
To: Top gear Production Group
Cc:
Subject: Tank-Top Gear pilot
Attachments: none

Verdana 12

From: Jennifer Pointishoes
Sent: 27 June 2008 15:12
To: Top Gear Production Group
Subject: Tank-Top Gear pilot

Hi guys,

I've watched the Tank-Top Gear pilot and I have to say I'm afraid
don't think this concept works. To me, it just looks like normal
Gear but in even more unfashionable clothes.

I'm sorry to be so frank, but really, I don't see what added valu
we're getting from making an entire spin-off show just so Jere
Richard and James can wear jumpers with no sleeves.

Best,

Jenny

Jennifer Pointishoes
Senior Commissioning Editor
BBC Entertainment

CANCELLED

BBC ENTERTAINMENT
TOP GEAR

CANCELLED

FAX

From: Top Gear Production Office
To: Mike Grunties,
The Big Top Company
Pages (including this one): 1

ust to confirm, we have
efinitely cancelled the rest
of the bookings for the big
top. After the first filming,
the BBC have decided not to
continue with *Big Top Gear*.
They found the show too
similar to normal *Top Gear*,
except it was in a massive
tent. Also, too many people
died.

Thanks for all
help.

BBC PREVIEW SCREENING

**JEREMY CLARKSON
RICHARD HAMMOND, JAMES MAY**
star in the new spin-off show from the
makers of *TOP GEAR*

CANCELLED

TELEPHONE COMPLAINTS LOG 27/04/08

BBC DUTY LOG

PROGRAMME NAME: *Top Ghee*
ORIGINAL TRANSMISSION: 20:00, Sunday 27 April 2008
TOTAL NUMBER OF COMPLAINTS: 493

SPECIFIC COMPLAINTS SUMMARY:

'I found this programme unacceptably fattening.' GF, Leeds
'This programme was pointless and greasy.' RS, Lancs
'A disgusting show, and very oily.' NW, Glasgow
'A complete waste of the licence fee and ghee.' SP, London
'A disgrace. Far too fatty.' ND, London
'I found this programme strange and unhealthy.' SA, Brighton
'The most oleaginous show I have ever seen.' IH, Devon
'Slippery nonsense.' AF, Notts
'Buttery and stupid.' HG, Birmingham
'This programme gave me indigestion. Awful!' WM, Surrey

THE ANIMAL CONTROL COMPANY LTD

TRANQUILISER DARTS....£5000
BEAR TRAPPING........£12,000
ENTRAILS CLEAR UP.....£4500

CASH DUE....£21,500

ORDER 604

Admit one
ednesday 6 May 2009
nsfold Aerodrome,
Surrey,

Terms & co

CANCELLED
being angry

Admit one
Wednesday 6 May 2009, Surrey, England
Dunsfold Aerodrome,

OVER 700 PEOPLE PUNCHED AT ONCE

TOP GEAR IS THE WORLD'S FOURTH MOST POPULAR TELEVISION PROGRAMME FEATURING VARIOUS STYLES OF TROUSER.

JAMES MAY HAS NEVER BEEN SEEN IN THE SAME ROOM AS AL PACINO. THIS IS BECAUSE MR PACINO LIVES IN AMERICA AND JAMES VERY RARELY GOES THERE.

TOP GEAR IS WATCHED BY 2.6 BILLION PEOPLE AROUND THE WORLD. THIS IS ENTIRELY CAUSED BY EVERYONE IN CHINA WATCHING EACH PROGRAMME TWICE.

RICHARD HAMMOND HAD A TOP 20 HIT IN NORWAY WITH HIS DEBUT SINGLE, 'I'VE JUST BEEN SICK IN YOUR HAT'.

SINCE SERIES TWO, EVERY EPISODE OF TOP GEAR HAS CONTAINED AT LEAST TWO REFERENCES TO EITHER SHIFTING SUBSISTENCE CULTIVATION TECHNIQUES, OR MEATS. USUALLY MEATS.

JEREMY CLARKSON IS SO TALL HE HAS TO BE FILMED SEPARATELY AGAINST A GREEN SCREEN AND SUPERIMPOSED ONTO THE FINISHED FOOTAGE NEXT TO THE OTHER TWO.

IN 2007, TOP GEAR DECLARED WAR AGAINST SWEDEN ON TWO FRONTS.

JAMES MAY ONCE THOUGHT OF SOMETHING SO COMPLICATED THAT HIS ARMS FELL OFF.

TOP GEAR IS NOT POPULAR IN GREECE. THIS IS BECAUSE THERE ARE ONLY TWO TELEVISIONS IN THE WHOLE COUNTRY, AND ONE OF THEM IS BROKEN.

IN THE ANIMAL KINGDOM, TOP GEAR IS MOST POPULAR AMONGST OWLS.

KNOW ABOUT TOP GEAR*

THE PART OF RICHARD HAMMOND IS REGULARLY PLAYED BY DIFFERENT ACTORS. FAMOUS NAMES WHO HAVE TAKEN ON THE ROLE INCLUDE AMERICAN OLDER LADY ENTHUSIAST ASHTON KUTCHER, TOP-HEAVY COCKNEY BARBARA WINDSOR AND, OF COURSE, THE ACTOR NIGEL HAVERS.

STATISTICALLY, THE AVERAGE TOP GEAR STUDIO AUDIENCE CONTAINS SEVEN PEOPLE WHO ARE QUITE WISTFUL.

JAMES MAY GETS MOBBED IN PORTUGAL, NOT FOR PRESENTING TOP GEAR BUT BECAUSE HE RESEMBLES THE LOGO FOR THE COUNTRY'S LEADING BRAND OF ROLL-ON DEODORANT.

THE ENTIRE 11TH SERIES OF TOP GEAR HAD TO BE RE-RECORDED AT THE LAST MINUTE AFTER IT WAS REALIZED THAT ALL THREE PRESENTERS HAD ACCIDENTALLY DELIVERED THEIR LINES IN WELSH.

JEREMY CLARKSON IS ONE OF BRITAIN'S LEADING AUTHORITIES ON TOAD MYSTERY.

TOP GEAR CANNOT MENTION ALAN HANSEN, FOR FEAR OF UGLY REPRISAL.

ALTHOUGH HE IS FROM BIRMINGHAM, RICHARD HAMMOND CANNOT SKY DIVE.

JEREMY CLARKSON IS THE ONLY TOP GEAR PRESENTER TO HAVE A PERSISTENT SKIN DISEASE NAMED AFTER HIM.

EPISODE FIVE FROM THE SEVENTH SERIES OF TOP GEAR IS BEST VIEWED WHILST WEARING A SPECIAL DEVICE.

JEREMY CLARKSON, RICHARD HAMMOND AND JAMES MAY HAVE NEVER ACTUALLY MET.

* BECAUSE THEY ARE COMPLETELY MADE UP

AMBITIOUS... BUT RUBBISH

Five of *Top Gear*'s favourite heroic failures

∽❦ MG SV ❦∽

When BMW gave up on Rover, a group of plucky Brummie businessmen bought it for 10 quid and started thinking about what would be needed to keep the company alive. Unfortunately, they decided it was this. The SV was certainly distinctive, what with all those slats on its body, and it drove surprisingly well, even if when Jeremy tried to powerslide one on the track he smacked his head rather hard on the roof. But the Brummie businessmen hadn't thought this through, because the number of people who wanted a car that cost as much as a Porsche 911 but – crucially – WASN'T a Porsche 911, turned out to be almost zero, and their company went belly up soon afterwards.

∽❦ Spruce Goose ❦∽

Howard Hughes was a wealthy industrialist, aviator and moviemaker who dreamt of making the world's biggest aeroplane to carry troops during the Second World War. Unfortunately, he was also a bit mad. This might explain why he spent so long making perfect every bit of his new flying machine, that the war was finished before it was. Nonetheless, Hughes carried on and eventually his huge baby was completed, as tall as today's Airbus A380 and with an even bigger wingspan, all the better to carry its eight enormous engines.

In 1947 Hughes himself took the new craft – officially called the H-4 Hercules, but nicknamed 'Spruce Goose' – for its first test flight, covering just one mile at a maximum height of 70 feet. It would be the only flight this mammoth seaplane ever made. The war was over, the US government was narked that Hughes had spent their money developing a troop carrier they no longer needed, and Hughes himself was still mad. The Spruce Goose was certainly ambitious. But it was also a bit pointless.

Phillips Multiplane

Horatio Phillips was one of the pioneers of aviation. It's just unfortunate that some of his ideas were basically a bit rubbish. His theory was that instead of a pair of wings, planes should have many smaller ones. Up to 200 of them. Phillips fiddled about with prototypes for many years until, in 1907, his final multiplane design managed to fly for a distance of 500 feet. Ideal for people who really only wanted to get to places such as 'just over there'. After that the multiplane idea went away. Which is probably for the best. If Phillips' theories had ever been proved correct, it would have made 747s look ridiculous.

DeLorean DMC-12

John Z. DeLorean was a lantern-jawed American hero with a history of success. But when he came up with the idea of an 'ethical' sports car, his ambitions turned to rubbish. First of all, he took cheques off eager buyers without having engineered any of the bits underneath the pretty stainless steel body, or found anywhere to build it. Lotus sorted the first bit by using their Esprit chassis as the starting point. Then the British government gave him a sack of cash to put a factory in Northern Ireland. All seemed well, until people realized the car was basically a wheezy lash-up and sales dried up. With no one left to bail him out, DeLorean got in deep with a money-making drug deal that turned out to be an FBI sting, and his car business went down the pan. Oops.

Tupolev TU-144

This, not Concorde, was the first supersonic commercial airliner to fly, and the first to break mach 2, both things that in themselves would be impressive. It's just what happened afterwards that marks the Tu-144 as a truly heroic failure. The Russians brought one to the 1973 Paris airshow to demonstrate their technological achievement to the decadent West, only for it to crash during a demonstration flight. In light of safety fears, the rest of the Tu-144 test fleet was relegated to hauling mail and freight across the vast expanses of the USSR. In 1978 another Tu-144 crashed and in 1983 the Soviet government ordered that the whole project be canned, with the existing planes to be used only for 'flying laboratory' work, whilst on the other side of the Iron Curtain the rival Anglo-French Concorde was now merrily whizzing back and forth across the Atlantic without a problem. Whatever the Russian is for 'That's not gone well', that's what they might have said.

TOP GEAR

Top Gear is now watched by a global audience of approximately eleventy squillion people. Mind you, that stat did come from Jeremy so it might be a bit exaggerated. Nonetheless, lots of people around the planet seem to like the show and in some countries re-runs of normal *Top Gear* just aren't enough to slake their thirst for three silly men cocking around with cars. That's why television companies across the globe have bought the rights to make their own note-perfect renditions of the show, but of course there are some differences, as demonstrated by this look at Mexico's Topos Gearos, presented by Javier Clarksono, Ricardo Hammondo and Jesus Mayo.

RICARDO

JAVIER

JESUS

AROUND THE WORLD

ORIGINAL TOP GEAR SAYS...	MEXICAN TOPOS GEAROS SAYS...
Tonight, three supercars on our track.	Tonight, three Volkswagen Beetles on a dust track.
At exactly 12:24, we arrived at our destination.	At exactly 12:24, we all went for a sleep.
Are American cars any good? To find out, we all went to the United States...	Are American cars any good? To find out, we tried to go to the United States, but they wouldn't let us in...
The question was, how much car can you get for £500?	The question was, how much donkey can you get for 2.3 million pesos?
James was going to be some time, so Richard and I went for lunch.	Jesus was going to be some time, so Ricardo and I ate what basically looks like a pile of sick with melted cheese on top.
And now it's time for the news...	And now it's time for a sleep...
We decided to crack on with our next challenge.	We decided it all looked too difficult and we would leave it until tomorrow. Or the day after.
Thank you so much for watching. Goodnight!	The programme is over. Wake up!

AY-AY-AY! ARIBA ARIBA! AND ON THAT BOMBO SHELLO...

VW CORRADO

A coupé based on the Golf doesn't sound very sexy. But wait. It wasn't just based on the Golf. Some bits of it came from, wait for it, the PASSAT. Oh yes. No, hang on, that's actually worse. But it didn't really matter because the end result was far greater than the sum of its parts, becoming one of the greatest coupés – nay one of the greatest driver's cars – of the 1990s.

The Corrado didn't arrive fully match-fit, offering only an adequate 16v model or a slightly weird G60 supercharged version, but as soon as VW got its act together and fitted the hearty VR6 engine, it all came together in one unassuming, but actually rather wonderful, bundle of Germanic goodness.

And here's a couple of Corrado facts you might not know. Firstly, since it was always more popular in Britain than anywhere else, the very last example ever made was right-hand drive. And secondly, after this last car had been delivered to Britain, none other than *Top Gear* executive producer Andy Wilman – in his former life as a television presenter – personally drove it back to the Volkswagen museum in Germany where it has lived ever since.

What he didn't tell them as he arrived to drop it off was that on the way over, the *Top Gear* director in charge of filming him had driven into the back of it and they'd had to pull the bumper back into shape. Rather than admit to this rather embarrassing faux pas, they just ran off.

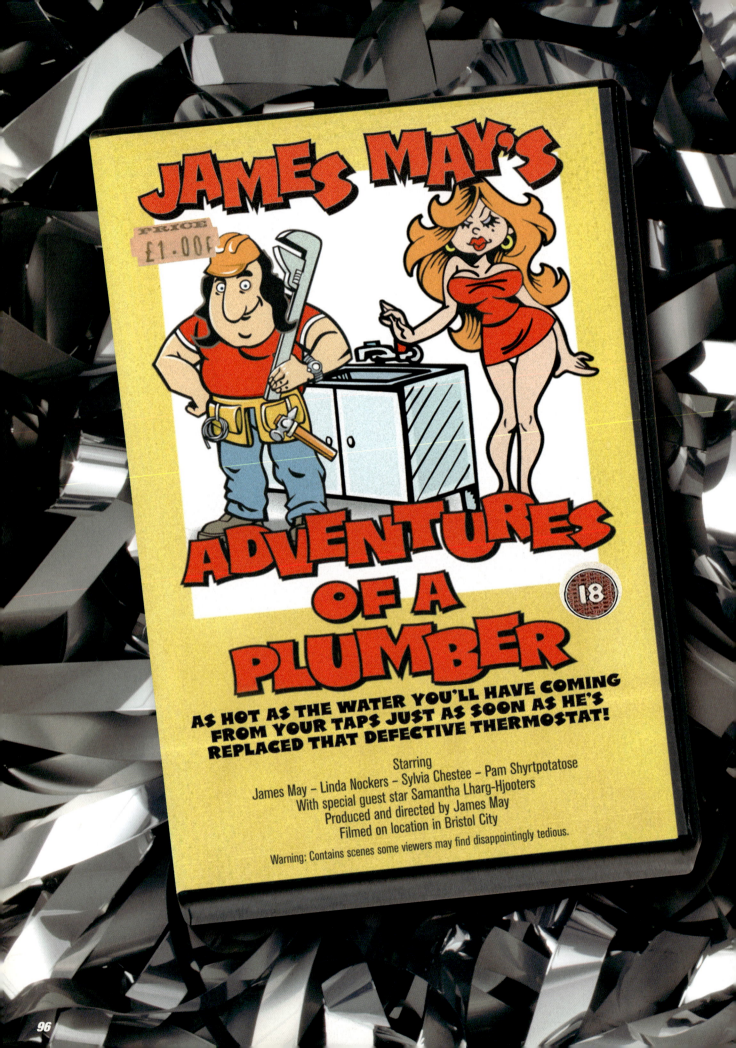

ADVENTURES OF A PLUMBER

Scene 1 – the front door of house

JAMES the plumber arrives at the front door and rings the bell. SUSAN answers. She is wearing a skimpy dress with stockings and suspenders.

JAMES
Hello. I have come to mend your boiler.

SUSAN
Ooh. You'd better come in then.

Scene 2 – the kitchen

SUSAN
Here is the boiler.

JAMES
Ah, yes, a Stottflow 370. These are notorious for niggling problems.

SUSAN
What are you doing?

JAMES
Removing the casing so that I can appraise the internal workings of your boiler.

SUSAN
But… oh dear! Some of my clothes have fallen off!

JAMES
Worse than that! Your main cooling fan is *extremely* clogged up with dust and fluff. No wonder you were having problems!

SUSAN
Oh Mr May, don't you want a screw?

JAMES
That's extremely kind of you to offer but I actually have plenty, thank you. Look, they're all arranged by size and type in this special tray that sits atop my toolbox.

SUSAN
That's not the kind of toolbox *I'm* interested in!

JAMES
I see. You'd prefer one of the modern plastic ones? I agree, they are lighter and in some senses more practical, but this old metal version has served me well for many years.

SUSAN
Mr May, would you like to see my jugs?

JAMES
I'm glad you mentioned that. If you do have a jug or some sort of other receptacle, I will need to borrow it if that isn't too much trouble as I fear I may need to bleed the main water reservoir. I will of course pour the contents down the sink once it is filled.

SUSAN
I've got something else that needs filling!

JAMES
Yes, I noticed that when I came in. Sadly, I don't do minor plasterwork repairs, but if that unsightly damage to the stud wall between here and your utility room needs attention I can recommend an excellent plasterer.

SUSAN
Ooh, Mr May, that's an absolutely massive one!

JAMES
Yes, it's called a torque wrench.

The Secret World of Top Gear dog

Sit! Ithangyooverymush. Ladies and gentlemen, TG Dog has left the building. Oh wait, she's just fallen asleep in the jungle room.

Top Gear is often asked, 'What ever happened to that walking carpet you had on the show a few series ago?' But rea... the question should be, 'What on earth wa... she getting up to before she became a lazy sidekick for Jeremy, Richard and James?'. These pictures help to shed some light on t...

Did he have WMDs? Maybe not. But it's a surprise to discover that he did enjoy the company of an idle, panting hearth rug.

Breaker, breaker, Tee Gee this is the Bandit. You got a smokey on your tail... oh no wait, it's just some soil from lying in the flowerbed.

The lady's not for turning. Well, certainly not to the right. Otherwise she'll trip over her slow-moving shaggy friend there.

He did not have sexual relations with that woman. But he did enjoy a good stroke with the fluffy bitch next to him. The dog, not Hillary.

'Hello, hello. With a dog called Tee Gee-oh.' That was the original lyric. Probably. Written at the same time as 'Beautiful Dog'.

Ahhh, *Top Gear* Dog seems to have nodded Hoff. She's drifted Hoff to sleep. Hope she doesn't try to run Hoff [that's enough Hoff puns thanks – ed].

THE TOP GEAR

```
V W F N J E R E M Y C L A K S N O R G O X T J O S Q W L S F
W K K H E G G O K U E H C W I Q W U B C A A W N G L E R U J
H V J F L A P S H O T E E T H W H I T E N E R Q O I H Y N T
E C S E L A W N I E V I L T O N O D I F B W B O U G 0 U A H
R J C J F P Y C V V V H M Y J I K T Z I S G C Y A 0 K S J E
E T O S G O Y T K X H O J N Y Q R S Q E A N U U 5 G U U A S
H H I B H C I E B R T R Q W U O A J G N U P Z 1 S F J B M T
A G D Z A O H R L R O I Q F H E O N D Y T U H O H P S Z E I
S N U V I O C R D I M R W U S D E O L N C C M P K W W E S G
J U T E B L P G R U N T I E S L N S H T A E L H F Z E R W I
A V S D E W K L L C E N B W L T U S U E S F P D O H N O A S
M D E I B A N C W O N D O A H O I M S A H K J R M D E W S ?
E S H L J L F S C K L L H A I B F U Y N T M G K V U H S F E
S O T S Q L X E Z A S C T R B P E D A N K C O C H O T G I B
G D O R M A A V P N F B E U M V K A E W O E X O B K O J R T
O N T E L Q S A I O O S R K A O X C A Z L O Y D C K D Y S I
T W K W K N Q A S M G T W G C B F J M V D I J I W E O Z T N
T F C O T Y P E B B U F S B E L L E N D H H Q P V R T J T A
O X A P R T I S S B X R U Z W N E F B P S Z A Z U A E S O C
? J B O A R H C S T E K N C A B E R H Z I H I J F S M O A D
R C U C E E R U D C L M D N O M M M M A H D R A H C I R R R
T S E S L F O T U V A Y D A C I A S A N D E R O Y O T L R A
K B A L Q I I D I N M S Y C M X Y Y T C V H Z A N B Q M I H
R V E V T K O L X V H Q T R A F T H H W I C P O P U M A V W
G C F I T R J L W G X T I M N S G G F A M A C U O K T J E O
M U B D P B Z X A ? P A L S I H E E S O T S T N A W O H W H
L M A E G Q N C I R D T H A T H A S N O T G O N E W E L L C
A C H E L L O A N D W E L C O M E B M K D L G H Q W W F J G
G T N L D R R W A I Y R E E E E E E W O P A O Z Q V Q A P
S R N C R U C I B L E O F M O T O R S P O R T S D Q Y I S B
```

Top Wordsearch

I found these very hard! Although in fairness, that's because I'm a dog.

Hidden within the grid above are words and phrases associated with *Top Gear*. If you find them all do let us know because we got The Stig's mate Kven Nnno to set it and you have to bear in mind that this is the man who organized that pub quiz where some bloke lost an arm.

PUZZLE PAGES

Spot The Difference!

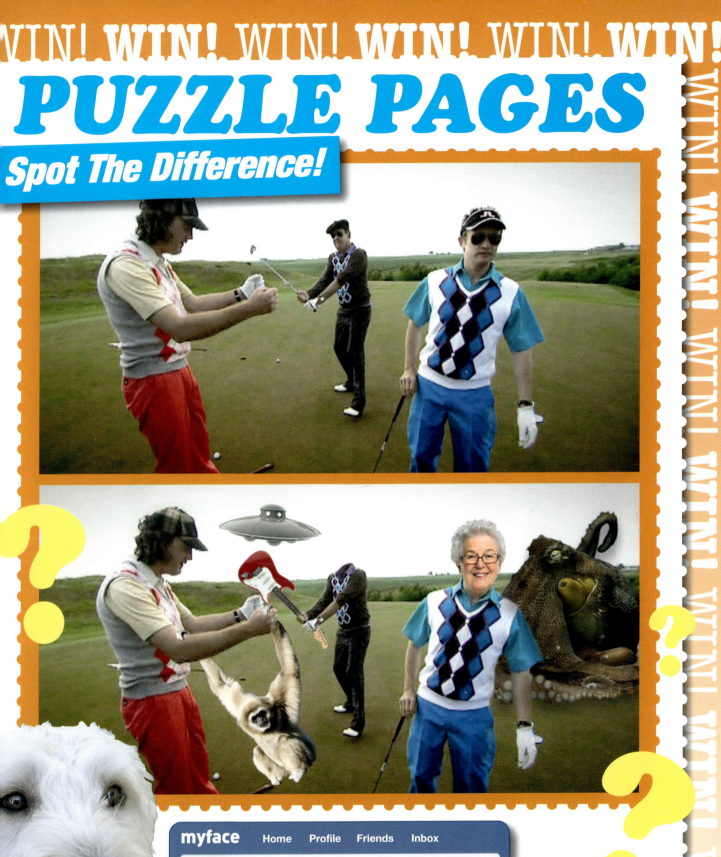

myface Home Profile Friends Inbox

Jeremy Clarkson is playing the drums. Stupid drums. Why won't they let me hit them in time? Damn damn DAMN. Plainly these drums are broken.
20 minutes ago · Comment · Like

myface Home Profile Friends Inbox

Jeremy Clarkson is going to learn the piano.
18 minutes ago · Comment · Like

THE SURREY BADGER

16 August 2009 • 85p • Your leading source of other people's wedding photos and small typing errors since 1922

Photo: Genericpicturesforlazylocalpapers.com

Recent record rise in car accidents finally explained

The large and mysterious rise in the number of car accidents that could be attributed to falling asleep at the wheel has finally been traced to the launch of a range of audio books featuring the popular *Top Gear* presenter James May.

The collection of CDs, entitled *Oooh, hullo – James May is Speaking Now*, was released in November last year and is said by its producers, Nasal Records, to have sold extremely well, both in the run up to Christmas and well into the new year.

In February, police and road safety groups expressed alarm at a sudden massive rise in the number of car accidents caused by drivers falling asleep at the wheel. Empirical evidence suggested the number of incidents caused by drivers feeling sleepy or actually falling asleep had risen by 1000 per cent in just two months.

The road safety group BeARD, in co-operation with police forces in Surrey, West Midlands, Lancashire and North Yorkshire, launched an immediate investigation which this week concluded that the dramatic rise is entirely due to James May's audio books.

'These books may initially seem interesting,' said BeARD spokesman Nigel Shuffle-Wheeler. 'However, there are a number of important safety problems with them. First of all, there is James May's voice, which is very pleasant and soothing. Secondly, there are the actual books being read out. There can be very few people who honestly want to listen to an entire repair manual for a Mark 1 Vauxhall Cavalier or the extremely detailed pre-flight checks and

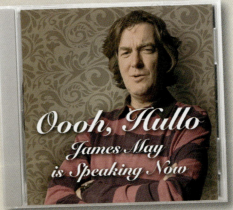

One of James May's culprit compact discs, yesterday

flight plan for a light aircraft traveling from Suffolk to West Bedfordshire in audio format.

Sadly, it seems some people have decided to stick at it, despite the huge risk of drowsiness once you get past the first four minutes and, worse still, they've been listening to these CD box sets in their cars. Frankly, it's a wonder more people weren't killed. Or just died through boredom.'

May's audio publishers insist their CDs and the rise in sleep-related accidents is entirely coincidental and they are quick to defend the contents of their controversial product. 'It is entirely wrong to suggest that James's CDs are just one man laboriously reading out lengthy and rather dull things that only he finds interesting,' said a spokesperson. 'Throughout every disc James enlivens proceedings by throwing in personal anecdotes of his own that relate to the literature he is reading aloud. In the Rover P6 repair manual 9-disc set, for example, there are over 24 different personal asides from James relating to the maintenance of these cars, each one lasting for at least 56 minutes'.

However, despite denials that the May audio books are not very interesting and really do go on a bit, Nasal Records has now agreed to insert a loud siren noise into each disc at five-minute intervals to prevent drivers from slipping out of consciousness.

PAGE 7: Baffling increase in number of people with black eyes traced to new Richard Hammond Nose Tissues.

THE POWER OF LITERALLY

Top Gear likes the word 'literally'. It helps to make sentences sound more interesting and urgent, and makes *literally* almost no sense in most of the contexts in which it's used. The keener-eyed amongst you will have noticed that we *literally* slipped an actual 'literally' into that last sentence. Actually, we *literally* did it in the next sentence too, and *literally* got two of them into the bit you're reading now. Wasn't that exciting? Didn't it make this entire paragraph much more interesting, even though grammatically and semantically it was a grotesque sodding insult to the English language? Yes my friends, that is *literally* THE POWER OF *LITERALLY*.

The good news is that by paying close attention to the tips below, you too can enjoy the POWER OF *LITERALLY* in your life.

For example, in normal conversation you might say, 'I am going to the shops'. But with the POWER OF *LITERALLY* that would become, 'I am *literally* going to the shops'. See how instantly this makes it sound more powerful and exciting?

The good news is that the POWER OF *LITERALLY* can be used on so much more than announcing a short trip to buy milk or hats or a thing that gets the rest of the blood out of the curtains.

Let's look at another example. In a dull and boring world you might say, 'You'll never guess what. I was walking past the Post Office when I saw the actor Nigel Havers getting into a red sports car!' Now let's try that again using the POWER OF *LITERALLY*: 'You'll *literally* never guess what. I was *literally* walking past the Post Office when I *literally* saw the actor Nigel Havers *literally* getting into a *literally* red sports car!'

Sounds good doesn't it? And the other joyous thing about the POWER OF *LITERALLY* is that it's so easy to use. Pretty soon you'll be unleashing it to spice up your sentences almost without thinking. But to help you get your eye in, here are a few more examples that have been *literally* given the zing that only the POWER OF *LITERALLY* can *literally* bring!

I *literally* love you • The kitchen is *literally* on fire! • I'm *literally* so sorry that I *literally* ran over your dog • That truck is *literally* rolling down the hill! *Literally* look out! • I think I have *literally* made a bit of a mess in your bathroom • I am *literally* giving you the money. Please don't *literally* hurt us • Is this *literally* the room for my divorce proceedings?

Top Gear aro

Since *Top Gear* is now the world's fifth most popular programme about deliberately crashing cars into things, it's only natural that other television stations around the world would want to buy the format rights and start making their own versions of the show. Sure enough, not long ago the main TG nerve centre in London received a telex from New Zealand proposing a locally-made version of *Top Gear*, in exchange for £104. The Kiwi spin-off has gone on to become a huge success with almost six of the seven people who own a television set in New Zealand saying that they sometimes watch the show and enjoy the exploits of Jez Clarkson, Rich Hammond and Jim May. But of course, there are differences between their programme and the UK show, as this handy chart demonstrates.

Rich

Jez

Jim

ORIGINAL TOP GEAR SAYS...

New Zealand Top Gear says...

ORIGINAL TOP GEAR SAYS...	New Zealand Top Gear says...
This week, the new Ferrari on our track...	This week, a nine-year old Mazda 323 on the road past the farm...
Is the new Lamborghini Gallardo faster than a jet fighter?	Is the Mazda 323 faster than a tractor?
And Tom Cruise is the Star in the Reasonably Priced Car.	And Neil Finn will be in the Mazda 323. Again.
How hard can it be?	Is the Mazda going to start mate?
That's not gone well.	Aww Jeez, you've dented the Mazda, Jim.
I was the first to arrive.	We all arrived at the same time, because we were in the same car.
We were ambitious, but rubbish.	We were ambitious, and you know it really wasn't that bad mate.
Join us next week when we'll be jumping the new Zonda over a pile of Koenigseggs.	Join us next week when hopefully Neil will lend us the Mazda 323 again.

That's it for this series. Join us again after the lambing season...

Get treated as a god amongst men by unfurling these top car facts

01 Porsche isn't just a sports-car maker. The company also has a very successful engineering consultancy business that designs and develops cars for other people, including, rather bizarrely, such sexy luminaries as Kia and Lada.

02 The old Triumph factory at Canley, on the outskirts of Coventry, was once so massive it was nicknamed 'The Rocket Range'. The whole place has long since been demolished, but the company's presence can still be felt in the area thanks to the roads on the new housing estates that cover the old factory land, which are named after its most famous models. Hence you'll find Herald Avenue, Dolomite Avenue and Spitfire Close. The Triumph name itself is now owned by BMW.

03 The Porsche 924 – which spawned the more powerful 944, much beloved by Jeremy – was originally designed by Porsche on behalf of Volkswagen. When VW got cold feet about selling their own sports car, Porsche took the designs back and stuck their own badge on the front.

04 When the McLaren F1 was due to undertake its mandatory 30mph crash test against a concrete block, the car's designer, Gordon Murray, was so confident of the car's strength that he asked if he could sit in the driver's seat during the test. The crash test boffins said no, but even they were amazed by how well the F1 resisted being smacked into a wall. So well in fact that, were it not for the headlights and front indicators getting smashed during the test, Murray could have happily driven the car home again straight afterwards.

3 second guide to...
LAMBORGHINI

Top Gear's quick* guide to one of the world's greatest car makers

LAMBORGHINI LP 500

Ferruccio Lamborghini was an Italian man who was extremely jealous of his neighbour Enzo Ferrari because Enzo made red cars with horses on them and got lots of girls, whilst Ferruccio just made tractors and only got to talk to Italian farmers with faces like a deflated basketball, so he decided to do something about it by making a car, and it would be lime green and have a bull on it, which would make it better than silly Enzo's cars, especially since Ferruccio had the ingenious idea of putting the engine in the middle like a racing car, so that he would be able to say to girls look at my lime green car with a bull on it, it's just like a racing car, and it turned out that many people who had recently made a few quid liked this idea, and so it was that Ferruccio's car-making idea was a great success, all thanks to Rod Stewart.

*Some might say too quick. And wrong.

106

TOP GEAR RESCUE

ANOTHER MARTINI HAMMOND?

ABSOLUTELY!

HONK! HONK! HONK! HO HONK! ONK! H K! HONK! ONK! HON K! HON

THE EMERGENCY ALARM!!! SOMEONE'S IN TROUBLE!

TO THE TOP SECRET HANGAR

LET'S GO!!!

HAIRSTYLE PUBERATION COMPLETE

COMMENCING FATERIZATION

SMALLERATING COMPLETE

COMMENCING MAD HAIR STYLERATING

GUYS... ...ERM... ...I SEEM TO BE A BIT STUCK...

POP!

THAT GOT IT. LET'S GET CRACKING!

110

FERRARI F40

Modern Ferraris are very good, but they're so slathered in computer technology and digital 'driver aids' that they can feel a bit nerdy. You imagine that if they could talk they'd do so in a nasal and annoying way that would eventually make you want to punch yourself in the face.

The F40 is different. Built to commemorate Ferrari's 40th anniversary, it was also the last car to be completely overseen by Enzo Ferrari himself before his death in 1988, just a year after the F40 was announced. And it is arguably the last pure, distilled Ferrari.

No traction control, no multi-setting differential, no steering wheel covered in switches and lights, no million-setting suspension system. Just a walloping 2.9-litre twin turbo V8 behind you and purely analogue steering, brakes and a normal manual gear change that do exactly what you want them to do. Magical.

OTHER STUFF WE LOVE...

TOP GEAR DOESN'T JUST LIKE CARS YOU KNOW. SOMETIMES THERE'S A TIME AND A PLACE FOR BOATS, PLANES, TRAINS AND LORRIES. BUT ONLY THE VERY, VERY COOLEST ONES. AND HERE THEY ARE...

LOCKHEED SR-71 'BLACKBIRD'

The stuff that *Top Gear* builds always ends up being a bit wonky and often on fire. But in Jeremy, Richard and James's minds – well, at least in Jeremy's – everything should turn out looking like this. Which is fair enough, because the Blackbird is quite simply the coolest plane ever made. Built predominantly from titanium, powered by what are effectively four ramjet engines and on record as hitting over 2000mph and capable of flying at 85,000 feet, the most amazing thing about the SR-71 isn't that it's still the most glorious and sinister looking machine ever constructed by mankind, although that is rather splendid in itself. No, the *really* amazing thing about this wonderful spy plane is that it first flew in 1964. That's one of the fastest and most advanced aircraft ever made, and it dates back *forty-five* years. But there's a depressing side to the Blackbird too because, like Concorde, it's now been retired and most of the remaining examples live in museums. Boo and, if you will, hiss.

OTHER STUFF WE LOVE...

MIL MI-12 HELICOPTER

This is *literally* the biggest helicopter ever built, a huge, twin-rotor beast confected by the Russians in the late 1960s to haul enormous loads, including missiles. Two prototypes were built before the Soviet military machine – deterred by a few teething problems – decided that it didn't need such a monster and the whole project was binned. The first Mi-12 is reckoned to be hidden away inside Mil's R&D facility, whilst the second (pictured) is on display at the Russian Air Force Museum in Monino near Moscow. Which is well worth remembering if you're in the area and find yourself with a bit of time to kill.

THE TORNADO

Nineteen years and £3m in the making, the Tornado is the pet project of a dedicated band of steam locomotive enthusiasts and their desire to build a brand new 'Peppercorn class' A1 Pacific train to fill the hole left when, unusually amongst old steam locos, every single one of the old 'Peppercorns' was scrapped back in the 1960s. The Tornado is completely true to its forebears, having been built to the original plans which were rescued from a skip when the LNER works were demolished. *Top Gear* loves this magnificent engine so much it became the star of series 13 with a smutty faced and exhausted Clarkson on the footplate.

LIEBHERR T 282 B

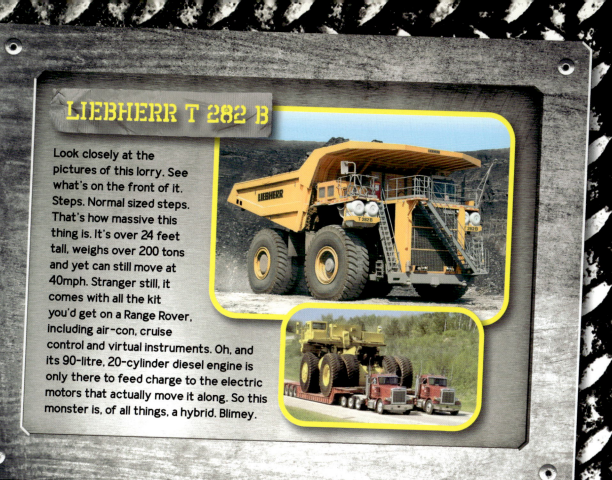

Look closely at the pictures of this lorry. See what's on the front of it. Steps. Normal sized steps. That's how massive this thing is. It's over 24 feet tall, weighs over 200 tons and yet can still move at 40mph. Stranger still, it comes with all the kit you'd get on a Range Rover, including air-con, cruise control and virtual instruments. Oh, and its 90-litre, 20-cylinder diesel engine is only there to feed charge to the electric motors that actually move it along. So this monster is, of all things, a hybrid. Blimey.

M80 STILETTO

The first thing you need to know about the Stiletto is that it was commissioned by the United States military's Office of Force Transformation. It's not entirely clear what this actually does, but it certainly sounds like an ace place to work. You just know they have extremely cool ID cards. The second thing you need to know is that this entire ship is made of carbon fibre. And, just when you thought the M80 couldn't get much more exciting, it's currently being trialled by one of America's elite forces, the Navy SEALs, who are sort of like the SBS but with more shouting. Probably. Oh, and the Stiletto can do 70mph which is pretty brisk for a boat. Admit it, you want one.

PRESENTERS' DRIVING TESTS

We all remember passing our driving test but, as we found out in series 13, only one of the presenters managed it first time. These documents shed light on what happened when Jeremy, Richard and James originally took their tests

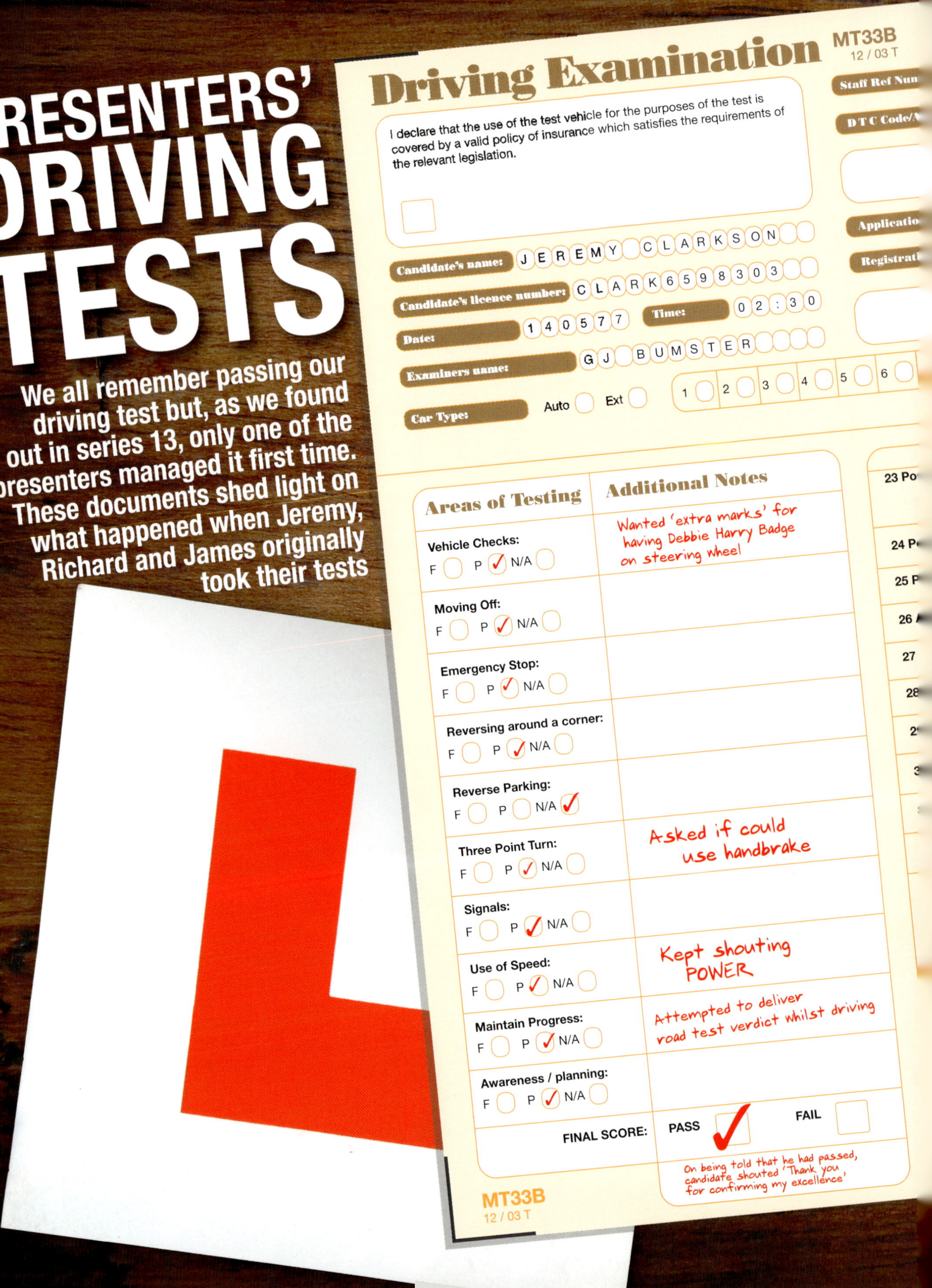

Driving Examination

MT33B
12 / 03 T

I declare that the use of the test vehicle for the purposes of the test is covered by a valid policy of insurance which satisfies the requirements of the relevant legislation.

Staff Ref Num

D T C Code/

Application

Registrati

Candidate's name: J E R E M Y   C L A R K S O N

Candidate's licence number: C L A R K 6 5 9 8 3 0 3

Date: 1 4 0 5 7 7   **Time:** 0 2 : 3 0

Examiners name: G J   B U M S T E R

1 2 3 4 5 6

Car Type: Auto ◯   Ext ◯

Areas of Testing	Additional Notes	23 Po
Vehicle Checks: F ◯ P ◯ N/A ✓	Wanted 'extra marks' for having Debbie Harry Badge on steering wheel	24 Pe
Moving Off: F ◯ P ◯ N/A ✓		25 P
Emergency Stop: F ◯ P ✓ N/A ◯		26 A
Reversing around a corner: F ◯ P ✓ N/A ◯		27
Reverse Parking: F ◯ P ◯ N/A ✓		28
Three Point Turn: F ◯ P ✓ N/A ◯	Asked if could use handbrake	2
Signals: F ◯ P ✓ N/A ◯		3
Use of Speed: F ◯ P ✓ N/A ◯	Kept shouting POWER	
Maintain Progress: F ◯ P ✓ N/A ◯	Attempted to deliver road test verdict whilst driving	
Awareness / planning: F ◯ P ✓ N/A ◯		
FINAL SCORE:	PASS ✓ FAIL ◯	

On being told that he had passed, candidate shouted 'Thank you for confirming my excellence'

MT33B
12 / 03 T

Driving Assessment Report

I declare that the use of the test vehicle for the purposes of the test is covered by a valid policy of insurance which satisfies the requirements of the relevant legislation.

CANDIDATE'S NAME: R I C H A R D H A M M O N D

CANDIDATE'S LICENCE NUMBER: H A M M O 8 5 8 3 2 0 1

DATE: 0 6 0 2 8 7   1 3 : 0 0

EXAMINER'S NAME: A L A N C A T F L I S P

CAR TYPE: AUTO ☐ EXT ☐

Moving off	✔	Excessively concentrating on showing off flames down side
Emergency Stop	✔	
Reversing around a corner	✔	
Reverse parking	N/A	
Three Point Turn	✔	
Signals	✘	Use of indicators was acceptable. Use of hand gestures to other motorists was not
Use of Speed	✘	Asked to 'proceed normally' approaching amber traffic light, shouted 'boot it' and accelerated through lights
Maintain progress	✘	Became quite angry when challenged on definition of 'proceed normally'
Awareness / planning	✘	Offered a 'punch in the knackers' if agreement not reached on what is meant by 'proceed normally'

Pass ☐   Fail ✘

Writing this whilst hiding in cupboard at driving test centre. Candidate is outside. Seems to be quite angry.

Licence Received: ☐

Ministry of Roads, Churches, Telegraph Communications & Hats. Form 2

VOLUNTARY DRIVING EXAMINATION FOR AUTOVEHICLES

Name: Mr James May
Date: 23rd April 1926
Weather: Unseasonably mild, don't you think?

Pre-driving checks: If anything, too thorough. Such business really has no need to take upwards of three hours.

Moving off from rest: Acceptable. Initially it was hard to discern if Mr May had actually commenced the setting off procedure, such was the initial lack of velocity.

Signals: Excellent. An especially impressive tip of the hat upon sight of a young lady.

Making progress: A concern. At some points during the examination we appeared to be making almost no progress whatsoever and Mr May had to be asked if he would please hurry up.

Politeness: Excellent. Extra marks were awarded for an especially jaunty wave to a Bobby on a bicycle as he overtook us.

Emergency stop: Upon being told that there was a (hypothetical) child running into the road ahead of us, Mr May responded simply that 'there was not', and proceeded as normal. This was the prelude to a somewhat pedantic debate which lasted for approximately two hours and thirty-seven minutes.

Examination result: Fail.

HOW TO HAVE A
TOP GEAR
CHRISTMAS

As with almost everything in life, there's a right way, a wrong way, and a *Top Gear* way. Which is mostly just the wrong way but with more hammers and arguing. So it is with Christmas. And the good news is that it's perfectly possible for YOU to have a *Top Gear* Christmas of your own. For example, why carve the turkey with a boring knife when you could use a chain saw? And why rely on predictable tree lights when, with careless use of a handy welding torch, you could light up the room with the warm glow of a flash fire? Yes, with a little application and a cavalier disregard for your own safety, you too can have a very merry Stigmas and a happy new poweeeeeer.

3 second guide to...
LOTUS

Top Gear's quick* guide to one of the world's greatest car makers

A bloke called Colin Chapman made himself a car out of things he had lying around in his garage and then, realizing that he had more stuff lying around in his garage than he actually needed to finish the car, sold some of the remaining stuff to other people and called it a 'kit car' before realizing that whilst some folks liked the idea of a badly made car they couldn't necessarily be bothered to throw all the parts together themselves because they were too busy smoking cigarettes so he moved to Norfolk and, having introduced local people to the idea of the wheel, he started doing the throwing together bit for his customers whilst also catering for their need to light fags with the philosophy that would later become his company's unofficial motto, 'add lighters'.

*And worryingly sketchy

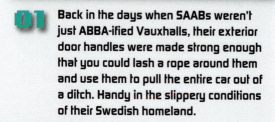

The follow-up to last year's best-selling OH NO, EVERYTHING'S EXPLODED AND THEN FALLEN INTO THE SEA!

CLARKSON IS BACK ON DVD!
AND THIS TIME HE'S BEEN
WELDED TO A TIGER

FOR NO READILY APPARENT REASON

FEATURING

FERRARI SCUDERIA SPIDER 16M!
How much G-force can it generate before the driver gets CRUSHED BY THE TIGER?

ASTON V12 VANTAGE!
Faster, more hardcore, but is there enough room to change gear without NUDGING THE TIGER?

ROLLS-ROYCE PHANTOM COUPÉ!
It's quiet. But is it quiet enough NOT TO WAKE THE TIGER?

PLUS

BLOWING UP A G-WIZ!
It'll annoy the environmentalists, but WHAT WILL THE TIGER THINK?

BUILDING THE WORLD'S FASTEST AMBULANCE!
Will it reach Jeremy before THE TIGER GETS HUNGRY AGAIN?

DAMON HILL SHOOTOUT!
How will Jeremy get on against a man who's faster, fitter and STAPLED TO A LEOPARD?

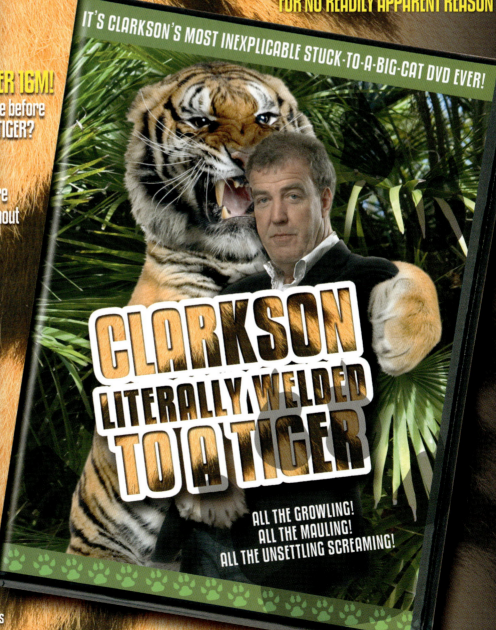

IT'S CLARKSON'S MOST INEXPLICABLE STUCK-TO-A-BIG-CAT DVD EVER!

CLARKSON
LITERALLY WELDED
TO A TIGER

ALL THE GROWLING!
ALL THE MAULING!
ALL THE UNSETTLING SCREAMING!

123

BENDY BUS FOR SALE. Some racing damage, hence £650. 01632 960564

LADA NIVA 4x4. The Communist car that's actually good. Except it isn't, hence £100. 07700 900652

AUSTIN-HEALEY SPRITE. Its NOT a Midget. Its bloody not. Clutch a bit broken, hence £1800. SOLD 0853

NISSAN 300ZX. Red. Twin Turbo. 4-wheel-steering. NOT ideal for ice racing. £1200. 03069 990040

RENAULT MAGNUM. Black, some terrifying impact damage, so £1000. 01632 960531

DAIHATSU TERIOS 4x4. Low miles, good condition, rare fox print job, some dog bites in body and interior, slight smell of fox wee, hence £5000. 07700 900875

AUSTIN ALLEGRO. Rare classic. Even more rare reverse jump damage. £250. Call 07700 900142, ask for *Top Gear* Stuntman.

Yes, *Top Gear* Stuntman. Look, it wasn't the best idea in the world but at least he's not on the programme any more.

PORSCHE 944 S2 . Classic coupé. Handles well, except on ice. Appears to say 'lesbian hat' on door, hence £600. 03069 990432

RENAULT AVANTIME

Rare track-car edition. Complete waste of everyone's time, hence £1000. 01632 960221

PROTON SEPTIC NAPPY . Vile Red thing with stripes up it. Buyer collects from dank tunnel near Parliament Square, assuming it's still there. £2. 03069 990897

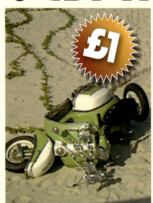

FORD FIESTA. 2008, 58 reg. Bright green. Some wetness and Marine damage, hence £6000. 01632 960221

HYUNDAI S COUPÉ . Red (mostly). Runs well. Slight exterior bodykit and impact damage. £200. 01632 960032

MG MAESTRO Red. Immaculate except for a small amount of massive rollover damage. £50. 07700 900142. Ask for *Top Gear* Stuntman.

WHAT DO YOU MEAN you don't remember *Top Gear* Stuntman? It was only about three series' ago.

FORD CAPRI. 2.8i. Smells funny, doesn't work. Buyer collects from middle of France. £200. 01632 960753

CITROËN AMI. French blue. Practical low-performance classic. Passenger seat belts slightly stretched by bosoms, hence £2400. 0~~SOLD~~92

DOUBLE DECKER BUS. Might have sort of fallen over a little bit, hence £400. 03069 990229

HONDA 50. Rather lovely. Not rare, hence £20. 07700 900264

If you have enjoyed this *Big Book of Top Gear* you might also be interested in the following:

The Big Book of Nigel Havers

Hammers and Hammering – A History
by O. F. Cockfayce

As You Do 2: Adventures With Nigel Havers, Nigel Havers and Nigel Havers
by Richard Hammond

A Brief History of Fire Extinguishers
by Alan Clisp

The Haynes Manual for the Triumph 2000 – A Companion Guide
by James May

The Last of the Summer Wine Annual 1984

Ha! George Bush Has Been Sick on the President of Japan
and 100 Other Great Moments Where People Sort of Fell Over a Bit
by Simon Cashin

Caravans On Fire – A History of Television's Least Contrived Moments
by Dr Samuel H. Manganese

Renault Avantime Tuning Manual – A Guide To Completely Wasting
Your Time and Everyone Else's Time Too
by Nigel Bisby and Lumsden Cress

The Basic Principles of Ice Driving
by Olivier Panis and Jean Wotisthishitbox

INDEX

INDEX

10 9 8 7 6 5 4 3 2 1

Published in 2009 by BBC Books, an imprint of Ebury Publishing, A Random House Group Company

Copyright © Woodlands Books Ltd 2009

Top Gear (word marks and logos) is a trademark of the British Broadcasting Corporation and used under licence. *Top Gear* © 2005

The Random House Group Limited Reg. No. 954009 Addresses for companies within the Random House Group can be found at www.randomhouse.co.uk A CIP catalogue record for this book is available from the British Library.

ISBN 978 1 84 607824 8

The Random House Group Limited makes every effort to ensure that the papers used in our books are made from trees that have been legally sourced from well-managed and credibly certified forests. Our paper procurement policy can be found on www.randomhouse.co.uk

Written by Richard Porter

Commissioning Editor: Lorna Russell
Project Editors: Caroline McArthur & Kelda Grant
Editorial Consultant: Michael Harvey
Copy Editor: Ian Gittins
Design: Red Giant Projects (www.redgiantprojects.com)
Creative Direction: Charlie Turner
Production: Antony Heller

Printed and bound in China
by C&C Offset Printing Co., Ltd.

BBC Books, *Top Gear* and Richard Porter would like to thank the following for their help in creating *The Big Book of Top Gear 2010*:
Jeremy Clarkson, Richard Hammond and James May, Andy Wilman, Adam Waddell, Martin Sharrocks, Ian Bond, Jamie Malcolm, Paul Presley, Angus Griffin and the team at Red Giant Projects, Cristina Dionisi, Julianna Nunn, Jim Wiseman, Giles Chapman and Lara Maiklem.

Picture credits:
BBC Books and *Top Gear* would like to thank the following for their help in sourcing and providing photographs and for permission to reproduce copyright material. While every effort has been made to trace and acknowledge all copyright holders, we would like to apologize should there be any errors or emissions.

BBC and BBC Worldwide Ltd. for all images apart from the following:

Jacket design by Studiospooky;

All other created artworks © Red Giant Projects unless otherwise stated; all car images © Giles Chapman apart from the following:

pp.11–15 Biggles May artwork by Bill Bradshaw/ Plum Dgitial Ltd © BBC Worldwide;

pp.50–1: Tom Cruise pictures © Getty Images for NASCAR;

pp.52–3: Le Man 24 Hour © AFP/Getty Images; Premier League © Matthew Lewis/Getty Images; Michael Parkinson © Getty Images Europe; German Pilot Gontermann & His Fokker DR-1 © Getty Images; US Airways Passenger Jet Crashes Into Hudson River By NYC © Getty Images;

pp.62–3: Alain Prost © Pascal Rondeau/Allsport/Getty Images; Nigel Mansell © Pascal Rondeau/Getty Images; David Coulthard © Ryan Pierse/Getty Images for Red Bull; Jodie Kidd © Emma Peios/WireImage; Sir Jackie Stewart © Mark Thompson/Getty Images; Robbie Williams © Mark Davis/Getty Images; Michael Schumacher © Getty Images;

pp.80–81 Garage artwork © Rod Hunt;

pp.90–1: The Spruce Goose © Bettmann/CORBIS; John DeLorean with His Automobile © Roger Ressmeyer/CORBIS; Russian TU-144 Aircraft © Hulton-Deutsch Collection/CORBIS; Early Aircraft © Hulton Archive/Getty Images;

pp.98–9: Elvis Presley © Bettmann/CORBIS; Saddam Hussein © AFP/Getty Images; Smokey and the Bandit © Everett Collection/Rex Features; Margaret Thatcher © Getty Images; Hillary Clinton, Bill Clinton and Chelsea Clinton © WireImage; Bono © Getty Images; David Hasselhoff © Getty Images;

p.108–111 Top Gear Rescue, p.64–67 Black Shadow and pp.8, 24, 73, 76 & 86 Zany World of Dr Clarkson artworks by The Comic Stripper © BBC Worldwide;

pp.116–117: Mil Mi-12 in flight © Erik Frikke; M80 Stiletto pictures © M Ship Co;

p.121: The Queen © ROTA/Getty Images;

All other images supplied by Shutterstock.com and istockphoto.com.